The Potter and the Clay

Jenny Kaluza

Copyright © 2014 Jenny Kaluza

All rights reserved.

ISBN: 172162032X
ISBN-13: 987-1721620326

Contents

About the Author 4

About the Study 5

Introduction 6

Week 1: Created with Purpose 8

Week 2: Center and Connected 21

Week 3: Air Bubbles 34

Week 4: Molded and Shaped 47

Week 5: A Lighter Load 60

Week 6: Nothing Wasted 73

Week 7: Mud is Messy 86

Week 8: Signed and Sealed 99

Week 9: Fragile Jars Of Clay 112

Week 10: Refiner's Fire 125

Endnotes 138

About the Author

Jenny Kaluza is a teacher, potter, author, speaker, wife, and mother. She and her husband, Zach, love raising their three (now four) adventurous children in the beautiful Pacific Northwest. Jenny's passion is to help women develop a deeper love for God and His Word. Her desire is to make the Scriptures knowable and applicable to every woman's life.

Jenny knew from a very young age that she wanted to be a teacher. She graduated from Whitworth University with a degree in education. Jenny served as the Children's Director for the Union Gospel Mission for five years where she taught all the school-age children. It was while she was teaching at the Union Gospel Mission that she first started writing. Out of a need for Bible study curriculum that would suit the needs of children who had been abused, neglected, and living beyond their years, Jenny started writing their daily studies. It became quickly apparent, that although she loves teaching in general, her true passion lies in teaching God's Word.

Along with raising her three (now four) children, Jenny enjoys teaching a weekly women's Bible study at her local church in Spokane, Washington. Through the loving support of women who saw a gift in her, she began writing women's Bible studies. Her first Bible study, *The Potter and the Clay*, focuses on the similarities she saw from her experiences of being a potter forming clay and God's interactions with humanity. She is also the author of *Living Hope*, an eight-session interactive study on 1 and 2 Peter. If you would like to learn more about any of her studies or other projects Jenny is working on, please visit her website at www.jennykaluza.com.

About the Study

The Potter and the Clay is a ten-session interactive Bible study which includes five days of homework for each week, as well as ten teaching videos. This study is designed for both interactive personal study and group discussion. All video sessions can be viewed at www.jennykaluza.com/the-potter-and-the-clay-videos.

I recommend allotting eleven weeks for this study. At your initial meeting, take time for introductions and getting to know the women in your group. You will then want to watch the first video *Created with Purpose*. After the video, you may wish to use the included group discussion questions to help facilitate conversation.

The videos for each week include clay demonstrations, as well as a teaching time. The videos introduce the topic that you will be studying in the upcoming week of homework. Therefore, the video and video discussion should be the last thing you do each week as a group. My suggestion for your group time would be to start by discussing your previous week's homework and then move on to the video and video discussion. Another option is to save the video discussion questions for the following week and discuss them when you discuss the homework. Since there are no group discussion questions for the homework, you could choose to go through each day of homework highlighting the important information and sharing insights with each other. During your final get together after you have finished week ten's lessons, I recommend getting together as a group one final time. This will allow you to discuss your final week of homework and view the video, *Putting It All Together*.

Although you are able to do this study on your own, participating in a group will help you to get the most out of it. Along with discussing the truths you are discovering, studying as a group allows you to pray together and build relationships. I encourage you to come to the study regardless of how much of the homework you are able to complete each week. Any time you are able to spend in God's Word is a blessing, and I don't want anyone to feel they can't come if they haven't finished.

Thank you for allowing me to serve you in this capacity. I'm so excited for you to meet God as the Potter.

Introduction

My journey into the world of pottery began my junior year of high school. I knew it was an art I wanted to continue so I signed up to take ceramics in college. I took every class they had and then became the teacher's assistant just so I could continue to get studio time. After graduating I taught beginning wheel throwing classes at our city's local Potter's Guild until I bought my own wheel and kiln for my home. Before having children, I worked full-time and pottery was just a hobby. As a stay at home mom of three kids, I was able to do pottery during naptime and some evenings. It became a small business that I could do at home.

As many of you may know, there are several songs and Scriptures that use the spiritual image of the potter and the clay. The interesting thing about pottery is that little has changed in the art since biblical times so those images still apply today. However, this is not an image that I initially identified with. It wasn't until I started spending extended hours using my wheel as a business, that I realized there was so much more to this art. You see, I am a perfectionist. The good, the bad, and the ugly, it is a character trait that has haunted me my whole life. Not all stereotypes are true of artists, but they typically are not perfectionist. This can actually run counter to the creative process. I will have an image in my head of what a piece should look like. When the piece does not meet my expectations, regardless of whether it could still be useful, it makes its way to the trash.

I have often questioned God in his wisdom as to why He would put such polar opposites in one person. I really think I would be much more productive as an artist if I was less of a perfectionist. I asked God, "Why have you put these two passions in me?" I heard a response in my soul like only God can give, "Because I am a perfectionist!" This response completely changed the way I look at pottery. God is the true Potter. I had been doing this art all along and had missed the most important part. This was not an income or a means to pass time; this was a relationship. This was an opportunity to see my God reveal Himself through one of the names He is called in Scripture. What did He want me to learn from this relationship?

The words potter, pottery, and pot are used in the Bible 77 times. The word clay is used 38 times. Any time God repeats Himself it is important to take notice. Why is God called the Potter? Why are we called the clay? What about that relationship is similar to our own? I set out to intentionally find the answers to those questions. As I have let God teach me over the last couple of years, I have been amazed how many lessons can be learned from the clay.

I was asked to share a small devotion on the potter and the clay at a women's event at our church. Afterward, one of the women came up and asked me if I had ever considered writing a potter and the clay Bible study. Of course, the answer was no. I tend to take on way more than I should, but this answer was clear. What kind of person just writes a Bible study? Little did I know that God was just using her as His mouthpiece. I went home unable to forget the conversation. The next day my chest was still pounding, and in defiance I went down to work on my wheel. I told God that our church has 10 weeks of Bible study. If He wanted me to write this study He was going to have to come up with 10 lessons. I started throwing clay and every time a lesson came into my head, I wrote it down. Guess how many lessons I had when I was finished throwing? In humility I called the women's ministry leader back and told her she was right. With some gentle prodding, I was encouraged to take on that task.

Like clay in the hand of the potter... In the spring of 2010, I finished writing the first draft of this study. In true Potter form, God was not finished with me or the study yet. It would take four more years and several hard lessons to get me to the place where I could complete this study. Thank you for journeying with me in the process. I pray you get a glimpse at the masterpiece He is creating!

      In His Hands,

      Jenny

Week 1
Created with Purpose

Day 1
Something Out of Nothing

Day 2
Tender Touch

Day 3
Finger of God

Day 4
Questioning God

Day 5
Reminding God

I am so excited to start this study with you. I love the beginning stages of working with a piece of clay. I can feel the clay squishing between my fingers. It is the feeling of smooth butter on the skin. I can smell the musty earthiness of the clay. The silence of my pottery room is comforting, and it provides sweet moments of conversation with my Savior. I am so excited to introduce you to the true Potter. During this first week of homework, we will look at the Creation of the Earth in comparison to the Creation of human beings. We will discover the personal and purposeful ways God interacts with His people and ways we can interact with Him. His care and attention to detail draw me closer. I can almost hear the hum of the wheel beginning to spin.

Session 1: Viewer Guide
Created with Purpose

Created From Dirt

1. _____ is just a fancy word for _____.

"I am just like you before God; I too have been taken from clay." (Job 33:6)

2. A pot has no _____ in the clay that was used. A finished pot points to the _____ of the potter.

3. We are always the _____. God is always the _____ (Isaiah 29:15-16, 45:9-13).

Pottery as an Art Form

1. Clay is a _____ material, incapable of beauty or _____ on its own.

2. Forming pottery is _____ and requires _____ _____ in its creation.

Purposeful Potter

1. The potter is the one in _____ and with a _____, not the clay.

Easton's Bible Dictionary defines sovereignty as God's absolute right to do all things according to His own good pleasure.

2. Only God can see things from _____ to _____.

3. God _____ all of His _____.

Video discussion questions

1. What are some things that are unique about the potter and the clay relationship that don't exist in other art forms?
2. In what ways does the clay bring glory to the potter and how is that similar to how we bring glory to God?
3. How can we bring glory to God without feeling devalued? (Saying, "All glory is God's and all I am is dirt" would make a person feel bad.)
4. How do we let people see the Potter in our accomplishments in a genuine way? How do we show off the process God is using to make us into something new?
5. Why is it unwise for the clay to tell the potter what to do?
6. What do Isaiah 29:15-16 and 45:9-12 have to say in regards to the sovereignty God has in dealing with His children?
7. Read Ephesians 2:10. What are we to God and why did He create us?

Videos are available for viewing at www.jennykaluza.com/the-potter-and-the-clay-videos.

Day 1
Something Out of Nothing

Here we are on the first day of a new study. An appropriate place for us to start is the first book of the Bible. No matter how many times you have read the story of Creation, there are always new things to pull out. Please begin by reading Genesis 1:1-19.

> In days one through four of Creation, what methods has God used so far to bring about His Creation?

We are not given a lot of details about how God made the heavens and the earth. One thing we do know is that all God had to do was speak and creation obeyed. Look back at verses 7 and 16. In these two verses we are told that God made something. The original Hebrew word for "made" is *asah*. It means "to do, work, make, produce, and accomplish."[1] This still doesn't tell us how He accomplished His creation, just that He did it. Let's continue with our passage. Please read Genesis 1:20-27, paying close attention to verses 21 and 27.

> What new word do we see in these two verses describing God's method?

It is not until God made living creatures that we see the word created. The original Hebrew word for "created" is *bara*. It means "to shape, fashion, or create."[2] This word refers only to actions by God. Only God can create something out of nothing. I love that it isn't until God starts making living creatures that we see a new word for His work. God is letting us know that He is involved in the process.

> When was the last time you did something creative? What did you make and what resources did you use?

I often feel creative when I am sitting at my pottery wheel. I love to think of new designs, textures, and shapes I can use in my pieces. I can make a wide variety of products out of a shapeless lump of clay. I then use fabrics, stamps, and household items to give further texture and interest to the piece. I can't think of a more basic and simple material to start out with than clay, but I still need the clay if I am going to make anything. No amount of planning and dreaming up designs will ever produce a piece of pottery without first having the clay. God is the only one able to fashion and form His creations out of nothing.

In Chapter two we get a more detailed description of the creation of man and woman. Please read Genesis 2:4-7 and 20-23.

What new details do you see in how God created Adam and Eve?

Yet again we get two new words to describe the methods of God's creation. In chapter 2 verse 7, God formed Adam from the dust. The original Hebrew word for "formed" is *yatsar*. It means "to form or fashion."[3] It is the same word used to describe the formation of a baby at conception. In chapter 2 verse 22, God made Eve from Adam's rib. Even though the word "made" may look the same as the other word "made" that we have already seen, this is an entirely new word. This original Hebrew word used for "made" is *banah*. It means "to build or rebuild."[4] This is the only time this word is used in the creation story.

With the creation of man and woman, we see a personal interaction from God that we have not seen before. God could have just given a command and human beings would have jumped to life. Instead, God became personally involved in the process.

What personal actions did God use to create Adam (verse 7)?

What personal actions did God use to create Eve (verse 21 and 22)?

God was not creating human beings from a distance. He breathed life into the nostrils of Adam, opened up his side to remove a rib, closed him back up, and formed Eve from the rib. I have no abilities as a nurse and can be quite squeamish so already these are more details than I needed. I'm so thankful God gives them to me anyway and pushes me past my comfort zone. As our days and weeks progress, we are going to see God get way messier than this. Our God is not one who is distant and out of reach. His method of creation is hands on, as well as His interaction with us. God desires to be personal with us and gives us glimpses of His nature right from the very first chapters of His Word.

Take some time to appreciate God's creation around you. What stands out and what do you appreciate the most? Take time to praise God for them.

Week 1: Created with Purpose

Day 2
Tender Touch

I tend to be a touchy-feely kind of person. The longer I know you, the more likely I am to reach over and hug you or put my hand on you while we talk. This works out great if you are also a touchy-feely kind of person. Thankfully my husband is also an affectionate person so I never have to worry if I am intruding on his personal bubble. However, my kids have varying levels of affection they need.

We use the idea of each person having an internal love tank. If you are filled up with love all the way to the top, your tank is at a 5. If your tank is completely empty, you are at a zero. Throughout the week we check in with each other by asking, "How's your love tank?" My oldest is a very kind-hearted and sweet little girl, but she does not need or want a lot of affection. Ninety-five percent of the time she will say her love tank is at a 5. All her needs are met, and she is good. My middle child is almost always at a zero. If I sit down for more than five minutes, there is a good chance she will be sitting on my lap. She is also the most likely to ask how everyone's love tank is since in reality, she is wanting to let us know she is in need of some snuggles. Our youngest is still too young to let us know his needs so he gets his love tank filled whether he wants it or not!

I think our Savior just might be an affectionate guy, too. Jesus was not one to just watch from a distance, but He sought out relationships and interactions from all who were near Him. Today we are going to look at just one aspect of His personal nature, the way He healed. Below I have several verses for you to read. Under each passage write the method Jesus used to heal.

	Matthew 8:1-4	Luke 17:11-14
Leprosy	_____	_____
	Matthew 8:5-13	Luke 13:10-13
Paralyzed/crippled	_____	_____
	Mark 5:21-24, 35-42	John 4:47-53
Close to death	_____	_____

At first, glancing through the gospels, you might think that Jesus spoke healing for some ailments and used a healing touch for others. I purposefully picked out healings of similar ailments so it would be clear that Jesus healed in multiple ways.

> Why do you think Jesus chose to speak healing in some instances and used His touch to heal in others?

I love a question that has no right or wrong answer but just leaves you pondering. There is no way to know for certain why Jesus used the methods He did, but I have my own ideas. Before I share those with you, I have one more miracle for you to read. Please read Luke 4:38-41.

What types of ailments did Jesus heal with His touch?

In verse 40 it says that people with various sicknesses were brought to Jesus. He laid hands on each and healed every one. We don't get a complete list of every disease He healed that day but He laid hands on everyone. We already know from the previous passages that touch was not needed to heal. He had the ability to just speak and a person would be healed. So why did Jesus also use touch?

I think Jesus used His touch to heal because He wanted to. I think if time and logistics permitted, He would have touched all who needed healing. I think Jesus likes getting in our personal bubbles and giving us the affection that we all so desperately need. How many of you are in need of some healing? As wonderful as it would be to have your prayers for healing instantly realized, how much more wonderful would it be to have Jesus' tender touch being the avenue for that healing?

Another reason I think Jesus used touch as an avenue for His healing was to shake up social norms. If you look at the list of diseases and ailments we know Jesus healed, there were many that would leave a person shunned from everyday life. Leprosy, menstrual bleeding, and dead bodies were all considered unclean. Those who were sick and in need were often not allowed within the city and certainly not allowed to socialize with the rest of the public. Those who came in contact with a sick person were also made to go through a time of cleansing before they could return to daily life. Not only was Jesus healing where large amounts of people could witness the miracles, but He was also touching them. I can almost hear the gasps coming from the crowds. This was not proper protocol. There is one story of healing that magnifies Jesus' use of touch and causes me to laugh just thinking about it. Please read Mark 7:31-35.

When was the last time you asked Jesus for something and He gave more than you asked?

Please tell me you are picturing this. Some people come to Jesus and they ask Him to lay His hand on a deaf and mute man. All they asked for was a hand; not even two hands, just a hand. Jesus says I can do better than that! I already told you I am squeamish, and here we have Jesus sticking His fingers into the man's ear, spitting, and then touching the man's tongue. Talk about getting into someone's personal bubble! I truly believe that Jesus would use touch to heal every time if He could. The healings that He didn't use His touch for were probably due to a greater plan being carried out, or perhaps their love tank was already full. Though I can't imagine anyone who couldn't use a little overflowing love from Jesus.

Day 3
Finger of God

The finished work of an artist always points to the skill of the artist and not the amazing talents of the resources that were used. Most artwork involves the use of an artist's hands. Whether you are a potter, a painter, a jeweler, or a seamstress, it is common to hear the phrase, "What talented hands you have." Artists are not the only ones with talented hands. Please read Psalm 8.

What does David call the work of God's fingers?

How does David respond after pondering the works of God's fingers (v. 4)?

Have you ever seen a piece of art that stopped you dead in your tracks? There was something so amazing, created with such craftsmanship that you had to stop and appreciate it. David found himself in that exact situation, but instead of an artist's work, he was stopped in awe over the work of God's creation. When David stopped to notice how majestic all of creation was, he suddenly felt very small. Rather than feeling insignificant, he marveled at how personal our Creator is with us even though He has made all things.

When was the last time you were struck with awe over God's creation?

Did your awe over creation lead you to any other thoughts? What were they?

Throughout the Bible when something was unexplainable or could not be repeated by humans, it was said to be the finger of God. This was another way of saying that something was God's doing. Below I have listed three passages that I would like you to read. After reading each passage, describe what action was attributed to the finger of God and state why it was attributed.

Exodus 8:16-19. What was attributed to the finger of God and why?

Deuteronomy 9:7-10. What was attributed to the finger of God and why?

Luke 11:14-20. What was attributed to the finger of God and why?

Now those are some talented hands! I find it interesting that something that clearly shows God's doing is called the finger of God and not the hand of God. Humans need their hands to make something amazing, but all God needs is a finger!

I am especially fascinated by the passage in Exodus. The magicians who were trying to convince Pharaoh that this plague was the finger of God did not even confess to having a faith in God. How interesting that even those who don't believe in God can still recognize His work. Simply knowing there is a powerful God does not always necessitate a desire to be with Him. How sad that they knew the art but not the Artist. For our last passage on the finger of God, please read Daniel 5:1-6.

Describe the scene taking place when the hand appeared and wrote on the wall.

What was the king's reaction to the hand appearing?

Next read the meaning of the message, Daniel 5:22-28. Summarize the meaning of the message in your own words.

Nothing will make the fingers of God appear faster than giving another god credit for His creation or messing with His kids. God does not allow the arrogance of King Belshazzar to continue. At the height of the feast, fingers appear out of nowhere and begin to write a message on the wall.

Why do you think God wrote the message in a language that they couldn't read?

Anticipation builds until finally Daniel is able to interpret the message. He lets the king know that the God who holds his life in His hand has sent the hand to write him a message. That very night the king would die, and the palace would be overtaken. I wonder if this is where we get the phrase, "The writing is on the wall." Oh, how important it is to recognize the work of God's fingers. Spend some time in awe over our Artist.

What are some things in your life that you can only credit to the finger of God?

Day 4
Questioning God

To start us off today, I would like you to reread some scripture that I had you read in our first session. Please read Isaiah 29:15-16, Isaiah 45:9-12, and Romans 9:20-21.

All of these passages show God upset by His people questioning His plan and purposes. He makes His point by comparing Himself to the potter and His creation to clay. In a simplified example like the potter and the clay, it is easy to see that the clay has no right to talk back to the potter or to question his ways. In fact, the example actually seems absurd. In this example, we can clearly see who is in control, and we don't question the potter's right to do as he chooses. When the comparison gets flipped and we are now the ones God is confronting for our challenging ways, it is not as easy to go along with.

    When was the last time you argued with God?

I tend to be an inquisitive and passionate person by nature. I always ask, "Why?" I also am not shy about sharing my opinion. My relationship with God is very personal. I speak to Him like I would a good friend, and I let Him know my feelings. I can clearly remember the first time I read the book of Job. It left me speechless and frightened. I will give you a quick summary of the book of Job, and then I'll share with you the passage that changed my speech.

Job was an upright and righteous man. God had blessed him with family and wealth. God knew him to be a man with whom no accusation could be found and He presented Him to Satan as a righteous man. Satan told God that the only reason Job blessed the Lord was because the Lord had protected him and blessed him. Satan retorted that if all those things were taken away, Job would surely curse God. God allowed His protection to be removed for a time. Job lost his family, wealth, friends, and health. Through all this persecution Job remained faithful and did not curse God. I cannot imagine another human being able to withstand the same amount of pain and fare so well. Though Job did not curse God, he did question His ways. For a sampling of the questions Job asked, please read Job 3:20-24.

    Summarize the questions Job asked of God.

    How would you describe Job's emotional state at this moment?

At this point in the dialogue, I'm right there with Job. I think he has every right to ask the questions he is asking. Death seems an easier path than the one he is on. He cannot see a purpose for his suffering and God has been silent. God will remain silent until we get to the final five chapters. Please read God's response to Job's questions in Job 38:1-5.

What is your initial reaction to God's response to Job?

My reaction was shock. I thought Job was doing so well, much better than I would have done. God's questions to Job go on for a full two chapters before He lets Job respond. Please read Job's response in Job 40:1-5.

Boy, can I relate to Job right now. Sometimes the only appropriate response is to stop talking and put your hand over your mouth! God then continues to question Job for two more chapters and then Job is given a final response. Please read Job 42:1-6.

Why has Job's attitude changed? What had he learned that he didn't know before?

I can barely read verse 5 without crying. We can have an intellectual knowledge of God, but we will never be changed until we come face to face with Him. How many times have I spoken about things that I didn't understand? Through Job's suffering, he came face to face with his limited knowledge, and his eyes were opened to see God's bigger plan. God loved Job, and He blessed the rest of his life even more than before.

I have to say after I read the book of Job for the first time, I was very leery to talk to God. I had spoken to Him with much harsher questions than Job. Surely I was going to be struck by lightning. God desires a personal relationship with us so there has to be a way for us to have an honest relationship with Him without offending. What does the rest of God's Word have to say about this? Did anyone ever question God without offending? Tomorrow we will explore this more. I want to leave you with some final questions to ponder.

Do we have a right to talk back to God?

Is there a respectful way to question God's choices?

Why was God angered by Job's questions and what could he have done differently?

Week 1: Created with Purpose

Day 5
Reminding God

As I shared with you yesterday, after reading the book of Job for the first time, I was nervous in how to best approach God. I didn't want some superficial relationship with God where I said one thing in my prayers but felt another thing in my heart. What should I do if the things I am thinking in my heart are not on track spiritually? Sometimes I have to just let some emotion out, and it is not always with sweet intent. It is impossible to hide things from God, but I also didn't want to question Him and then reap consequences. Thankfully, there are plenty of questioning people in the Bible from whom I could glean insight. There are several bold people in the Bible that laid their hearts bare before the Lord and asked questions. Rather than being offended, the Lord responded positively to them and gave them what they asked.

David is one of my favorite people in the Bible. He showed emotion, and he danced before his God with enthusiasm. If he had a thought or a feeling, he shared it openly with God. Most of the Psalms are written by David. In them are many questions he asks God, but not all of them are phrased positively. Please read Psalm 22:1-5.

What questions did David have for God?

Are there any differences between Job's questions yesterday and David's today?

Why did David's attitude change in verses 3 through 5?

David never forgot who His God was. He questioned what God was doing but immediately submitted to His authority and placed his trust in Him. David's words can seem a bit like an emotional roller coaster, but through his questioning process, he always comes back to the truth he knows about God. David could honestly share his questions with God because he had already committed to submission.

Asking God questions is one way I see people respond to disappointments in the Bible, but there is also another unusual response. In several situations, the people of God responded to their distress by reminding God who He is. Doesn't God already know who He is? Why would this method be effective? Please read Isaiah 64:7-9.

What does Isaiah want God to remember?

Do you think God needed a reminder? What purpose did these reminders serve to Isaiah?

God never loses sight of who He is but we do. Sometimes by reminding God who He is, we remember those qualities as well. Isaiah tells God that He is their Father and the Potter. Israel had gone off track from the covenantal relationship they were meant to have with the Lord. Isaiah reminds God that Israel is the clay and they are still His people. Isaiah was begging for God's mercy by reminding God what simple creatures humans are in comparison to His greatness. Sometimes by speaking the truth, our hearts are changed. Israel was the one who needed the reminder of who they were in comparison to God. Moses also liked to remind God who He was. Please read Exodus 33:12-23.

What were Moses' concerns?

What did Moses ask God to remember?

Why do you think Moses was able to ask such bold things from God?

Previously in this chapter, God had told Moses that He would not be going into the Promised Land with His people because they were a stiff-necked people, and He might destroy them on the way. Moses had these thoughts in his head when he was worried about how he would lead these people.

What does God say to Moses in verse 14, and how does Moses respond in verse 15?

Moses is so worried about going alone that he doesn't even hear God telling him that He will go with them. When Moses finally hears that God is in fact going with His people, Moses makes a bold request.

What does Moses request from God?

We will miss out on seeing God move in big ways if we are too afraid to ask for big things. God wants nothing more than to reveal His glory to His children. Go ahead, remind God of who He is and of the promises that He has made to you. As a result, you may come to believe those very things for yourself and get a glimpse of His glory!

Week 2
Centered and Connected

Day 1
Wrestling God

Day 2
Abide in His Love

Day 3
Buried Treasure

Day 4
Serving Side by Side

Day 5
The Road Back Home

Ladies get out those dumbbells; we need some muscles this week. The process of centering our lives to Christ takes discipline and focus. This life of faith is not for the weak. We have a choice of whether we are going to abide in Christ or wrestle with Him. There are several things that can help us keep on track and encourage us in our journey with Christ. For those who get off track, there is always a road leading back to God but it will take determination. Please join me this week as we discover the many ways we are centered to our Savior.

Session 2: Viewer Guide
Centered and Connected

Centering Our Lives to Christ

The initial centering of a pot is the most physical. As we go through life with Christ there are always two ways to do everything.

1. We can remain _____ to Christ and experience the _____ of that relationship.

Or

2. We can follow after our _____ _____ and experience the _____ of recentering (discipline).

The Vine and the Branches

The only way we can stay centered is by remaining connected to the Potter (John 15:1-17).

1. Fruit is when the _____ _____ is reproduced in the _____.
2. The gardener cuts off _____ branches any _____. Dead branches = _____ (vs. 2 and 6).
3. The gardener prunes off branches that _____ _____ so they will be even more _____ (vs. 2).
4. Pruning happens before a _____ _____ _____.

Deciding Where to Prune and Where to Grow

Evaluate where you can bear more fruit and what areas you have reached your potential.

1. Identify your _____. Ask yourself these questions.
    A. When do I feel _____ _____?
    B. What are my _____, _____, and _____?
    C. What has God given you a _____ for?

Week 2: Centered and Connected

2. Draw out your _____.

Things That Keep Us From Pruning
1. Branches bearing _____ _____ are more difficult to prune than branches bearing _____ _____.
2. Concerns that no one else _____ _____ or the program will _____.

Result of Pruning
1. _____ will follow.
2. _____ of fruit will _____.

The goal of staying connected to Christ is that the amount of fruit and quality will increase.

Fruit that will _____ is our goal!

Video discussion questions
1. God recenters us either through discipline or pruning. What is the difference between these two methods?
2. What are some reasons why God would want to remove some things from our lives, and what are some things He might remove?
3. What are some branches in your life that are difficult to prune?
4. Have you ever experienced the blessing of pruning in your life? What was the fruit that followed?
5. What are some examples of fruit that will last (eternal fruit) in your life?

Videos are available for viewing at www.jennykaluza.com/the-potter-and-the-clay-videos.

Day 1
Wrestling God

When I first learned to do pottery in high school, it was from a teacher who was a general art teacher and not a potter. She gave us general guidance, and we experimented on our own. I went on to take pottery in college and found I had learned several bad habits. The lead teacher was a man who could simply hold out one hand and center the piece of clay through sheer strength. I tried this method without success. I simply wasn't strong enough. The teacher's assistant was a woman who saw me trying to center my pot and said, "It looks like you are trying to wrestle the clay." I was in fact trying to exhort my power over that piece of clay. It was then that she demonstrated to me that my job was not to apply force to the clay but to remain in one place and let the clay come to me. Once I learned proper technique, centering became easy. The potter's job is to remain constant. The clay will continue to wrestle for a time, but the potter maintains that constant boundary. Soon the clay will spin smooth as it conforms to the hand of the potter.

Most Christians will experience times of wrestling with God. I suppose it is possible to smoothly walk beside God your entire life, but for those of us with a stubborn streak, some wrestling is required. Just as it is with the clay, I have experienced moments of wrestling with God when I was not willing to conform to the boundary He had placed. The Bible records a wrestling match between God and the patriarch Jacob. Please read Genesis 32:22-32.

The context of this story is important. Jacob had struggled with man his whole life, first with his brother Esau and later Laban. Now Jacob would wrestle with God. His family and servants had already crossed the river and were headed to the Promised Land. Jacob alone remained behind. This wrestling match is a turning point in Jacob's life. Before he could enter the Promised Land, he had some wrestling to do.

> What time of day did the wrestling take place (v. 22)? How would the time of day affect the match?

> How long did Jacob and his assailant wrestle?

> If Jacob would have known that he was wrestling with God, do you think he would have continued?

> What do think it means in verse 25 that the man could not overpower Jacob? Why did he injure Jacob's hip?

Since we have read the entire passage, we know that Jacob was wrestling with God. Why then would it say that God, in the form of the man, could not overpower Jacob? The original Hebrew word for "overpower" is *yakol*. It means "to overpower, prevail, overcome, have power, be able to gain or accomplish, and be able to reach."[1] It was not that God was not powerful enough to overtake Jacob, but rather Jacob would not relent. Nothing had yet been accomplished or changed in Jacob. God then gives Jacob a supernatural blow to the hip. Now, whether he wanted to or not, Jacob was unable to do things with his own strength. Jacob's eyes were opened, and he realized the blessing that he desired could only come from God. Jacob would not let go until God blessed him.

Rather than just give Jacob the blessing he requested, God asked him a question. What did He ask?

Before Jacob could receive a blessing, he had to say his name. In the Old Testament, a person's name revealed their character and nature. Jacob had to acknowledge that his name was "heel-catcher."[2] All throughout his life he had been relying on his own strength. In order for Jacob to be able to lead his people, that would have to change. God changed his name to Israel. By changing his name it implied that his nature and character had changed. The name Israel means to "fight with God and overcome."[3] Since this was also the name for God's people, it represented hope that they too would overcome and that God would fight for them. They would enter the Promised Land not on their own strength and will but by the power of God. This encounter forever changed Jacob. From this moment forward, he would rely on the strength and blessing of God.

When was the last time you tried to do something in your own strength? How did that work out?

What ways do you see God changing your nature?

We can choose to accept the boundaries and will of God or we can wrestle with Him. Wrestling happens when we are not aligned with the Potter, when we are trying to do things on our own. God will enter onto the mat with us and let us work some things out, but just as was the case with Jacob, wrestling can lead to injuries. You can only make a pot if the piece of clay is first centered. Lean into Jesus and conform to the hand of the Potter!

Day 2
Abide in His Love

In our last session, we read the passage of the vine and the branches from John 15. I only had time to show you how pruning keeps us centered, but today we will explore how abiding in God's love also keeps us centered. Please read John 15:9-10.

Depending on which translation you are reading, you will either see the word "remain" or "abide." The original Greek word for "abide" is *meno*. It means "abide, remain, continue, not to depart, dwell, and endure."[4] To get a full understanding of the meaning of this word, we will need to look at several verses that tell us to abide in Christ. We will look at three distinct actions that result in the believer abiding in Christ.

What must we do according to John 15:10 to abide in Christ's love?

Obedience to God's commands is a key action required for us to abide in Christ. Turn to John 6:52-58, but keep something in John 15 as we will be coming back there soon.

What action is Jesus implying by the words, "Whoever eats my flesh and drinks my blood abides in me?"

For a moment, I would like you to imagine being a Jewish person and hearing Jesus say these words for the first time. It was clear according to their law that they were never to drink blood. They also were very familiar with the concept of blood atoning for their sins. Here Jesus combines the two concepts and tells them in order to have forgiveness of their sins, they need to partake of His blood. Can you feel the shock waves? Jesus is the bread of life, and the only way we can have eternal life is if we partake.

The last action that leads to abiding in Christ is found in both John 8:31 and 1 John 2:19 and 24. In John 8:31-32, depending on your translation, you may see the word "continue" or "hold" in place of "remain" or "abide." The Greek word is the same, it has just been translated differently. Please read John 8:31-32 and 1 John 2:19 and 24 and answer the following question.

What action is necessary for abiding in Christ?

These verses talk about a continued belief, perseverance, and endurance. Once we believe, we must hold on to those things we know to be true and then the truth will set us free (8:32). So now that we have looked at all three actions that lead to abiding in Christ, let's put them all together.

Week 2: Centered and Connected

What three actions lead to our ability to abide in Christ?

Which one of these actions is the most difficult for you?

For some, the initial action of putting their faith in God is the most difficult. Once they have come to terms with the reality of Christ and put their faith in Him, the rest comes easier. Their belief is now certain, and they want to follow Him. For others, the initial belief was easy but the realities of life cause doubt to rise. It is a struggle for them to hold on to the truth that they know and not be pulled away by every new argument. Still for others, they believe and hold on to the truth but choosing to walk in obedience daily is difficult. The desire to be in control and lean on their own understanding can be a strong pull.

There is a beautiful benefit to all who are able to believe, endure, and obey. Not only will we abide in Christ through these actions, but there is another result as well. Please read John 6:56.

Not only do we abide in Christ as a result, but what also happens?

Ladies take a moment to soak that in. We abide in Christ, and He abides in us. What glorious communion!

I want to end today by going back to our passage in John 15. Please read verses 7 and 8.

What is the byproduct of continuing to abide in Christ according to verse 8?

The amount of fruit that flows out of our lives increases the more we abide in Him. The more time we spend with Jesus, the more our actions look like His. Have you ever had a good friend that the more time you spent with her the more you started to look and sound alike? I love listening to accents, and I pick them up rather easily. Since I am from the Pacific Northwest, the most accent neutral area of our country, I can easily look like a wanna-be. I will come home from an evening out and my husband will instantly know who I was with just from my newly acquired drawl. To make matters worse, I studied Spanish for several years so whenever I hear someone speaking with an accent, my brain instantly switches to Spanish. It doesn't matter if they are from Italy or France, they must need me to speak in Spanish! How embarrassing!

I can't imagine a friend I would rather look or sound like than Jesus. I think I might just tarry here a little longer and pick up an accent that might actually do me some good.

Day 3
Buried Treasure

There are so many things in this world that vie for our attention and easily get us sidetracked. The longer it takes for Christ to return, the harder it is to keep our hope firmly fixed on that promise. We can grow anxious in waiting and then the distractions seem even more appealing. In order for our lives to remain centered on Christ, we need to faithfully serve the King in His absence. Our service to Him will help keep our lives focused and our hope a certainty.

Our three children are still quite young. They have not mastered the skills of deception that unfortunately come with age. When I give them a task, such as cleaning their room, they are more likely to stay focused on the task if I am in the room with them. If I leave, the cleaning quickly turns into playing. Things that they would never consider doing if they knew I was watching are suddenly commonplace. The longer I am gone, the more atrocious the offenses become. Eventually, the playing turns into crying and someone gets hurt. I would like to think that these tendencies disappear with age, but unfortunately that is not the case. We just get better at hiding our disobedience. Please read Luke 12:35-48.

When did the servant's behavior get off track (v. 45)?

Why was the punishment more severe for the servant who knew the master's will and didn't do it, than the servant who didn't know the master's will and still did evil?

Why does God require more of those who have been given much?

What helped to keep the servants on task (v. 35-37, 42-43)?

One thing I want to clear up before we go any further with this parable is that just because the servant knew the master's will does not mean that the servant represents a saved Christian. We can have a great understanding of the Scriptures and never commit our lives to God. God holds us accountable for what we know and what we do with that knowledge.

I want us to pay close attention to the things that helped the servants stay on task and the things that got them off track. In both situations the master returned later than when the servants expected. The servants who were prepared when their master returned never stopped doing the tasks that were expected of them. They were in a constant state of readiness. They continued to do the tasks the master had assigned them even in his absence (v. 43).

The servants who were found disobeying the master did not start out that way. It was when they stopped doing the tasks assigned to them that they got in trouble. They no longer expected the master to return so they turned to their own agenda and selfish desires. It is the reality of Christ's return that will help us keep focused and ready. I have one more parable for us to read. Please read Matthew 25:14-30.

What similarities do you see between the parables in Luke and Matthew?

What are some examples of putting our talents to work?

Why was burying the talent met with such anger from the master?

At first glance, it seems like God is against the underdog. Why would those with nothing have everything taken from them and given to those who already have much? It sounds a bit like robbing from the poor to give to the rich. Our Robin Hood is a bit mixed up. We will learn the heart of this parable by studying the intentions of the servant with only one talent.

The way this master treats his servants is no different than how we develop trust with others. If you are going on a long trip, would you give your house keys to a stranger? No, rather you would give your keys to someone you already know you can trust in your absence. You might give a stranger smaller tasks as a way to build your trust. Perhaps they gather your newspaper and water your lawn. If those tasks were completed with care, you might trust them with a more important task the next time you leave.

The servant with only one talent dug a hole and hid his master's money. He buried the money not to protect it but to hide it. This servant did not expect his master to return. If he would have invested the money in the bank, the money would have been under the master's name and the servant would have no claims to it. By burying the money, if the master did not return, the servant could keep the money for himself. He chose to do nothing with the money and wait to see what would happen. The message of this parable is that those who wisely use what they have been given will be given more. Those who do nothing with what they have been given, even the little they have will be taken away.

We are the servants living in the time when our Master is away. When He returns, will He find us anxiously waiting and using our talents or distracted, disobedient, and wasting what we have? Christ's return is a certainty. Let us continue to do the good work He has entrusted to us with our eyes fixed firmly on the horizon.

Day 4
Serving Side by Side

I grew up in a large family. Since I was the oldest of six kids, there was always much work to be done. I'm sure you have heard the phrase, "Many hands make light work." This is true if all the hands are focused on a common goal. If there is no unity in purpose, many hands make chaos.

God intended the church to be the perfect picture of unity. When all the members are focused on a common goal, something beautiful happens; God is glorified. I clearly remember the first time I stepped into church as a junior in high school. My parents had taught us about Jesus, but I had never been part of the corporate body of Christ. I was overflowing with emotions. I had the strangest feeling that I belonged there. My feelings of belonging were not due to my ability to fit in. I had a very limited understanding of Scripture, and I was surrounded by kids who had grown up in the church. I remember the youth group was studying from the book of Ephesians, and I couldn't even find that book in my Bible. Rather, my feelings of belonging were due to the connection we all had based on the Holy Spirit residing within us. There was no way I would ever leave this new home.

This world is full of things that distract and pull us away from our relationship with Christ. The church, which is made up of all the believers in Christ, is a crucial part of keeping us centered on Christ. We need each other! Please read Romans 12:1-8.

> **Describe a time that you have been part of the body of Christ and something great was accomplished.**

> **Why was it necessary to have multiple people involved?**

> **In verses 4 and 5, Paul describes the church as similar to the human body. What similarities does he make?**

This chapter begins by Paul urging us to "offer our bodies as living sacrifices." This action is considered a spiritual act of worship. There are several ways our bodies become living sacrifices since they are the temple of the Holy Spirit (1 Corinthians 6:19). In this chapter, Paul speaks of our bodies being living sacrifices in the same context of all believers being part of one body. How do our bodies become living sacrifices in relation to the body of Christ? Romans 12:5 is a key to understanding this. We belong to all the other members. Christ, in His wisdom, did not give all spiritual gifts to any one person. Rather, we are dependent upon others' gifts if we are to function as a body. Since we are all dependent upon each other, no one should think of themselves as better than anyone else (v. 3). Paul uses the word sacrifice because giving of ourselves is not always easy.

Week 2: Centered and Connected

We may not feel like sharing our gifts. It is an act of worship when we put aside our interests and serve the greater good.

Based on Paul's statements in verse 3, some members were placing greater importance on certain gifts. Paul addressed this same problem in another one of his letters. Please read 1 Corinthians 12:12-31.

> What value is placed on the weaker parts according to verse 22?

Here again, we see that certain gifts were seen as more important. Specifically, in the city of Corinth, the gift of tongues was held in high esteem since it was such a showy gift. Paul, however, placed greater importance on the gifts perceived as less desirable because they benefited the entire body.

> Please read 1 Corinthians 12:11. Who decides who gets which gifts?

We cannot change which spiritual gifts we have been given. God gives as He determines best to serve His purposes. We will function best as a body when we appreciate the gifts of others and use the gifts we have been given.

My husband Zach and I are complete opposites. This could lead to frustration and annoyance if we let it. Instead, we have seen God do far greater things through our teamwork than either one of us would be able to accomplish on our own. When we see our gifts working together, we gain a greater appreciation for our differences and unique giftedness.

I want you to pay close attention to the verses that follow both of the passages we have read today. Please read 1 Corinthians 13:1-3 and Romans 12:9-13.

> What message do both of these passages have in common?

> Why do you think the message of love follows passages of the body of Christ?

It is impossible for a believer in Christ to possess every spiritual gift. We are, however, all able to have the fruit of the Spirit which begins with love (Galatians 5:22). It is impossible to serve the other members of the body without love. Without love, all the other gifts are meaningless. Let's face it, we can all be a bit cantankerous at times. Being part of the body means putting up with messy people, present company included. The love we have in our own strength will diminish quickly. We need the love that only the Holy Spirit can provide. Go ahead and ask Him for it! No one loves the church more than Jesus.

Day 5
The Road Back Home

For several days we have talked about things that help keep us centered and connected to Christ. What happens if you have wandered away? How do you recenter your life to Christ? Fortunately, the Bible has a lot to say about that, too. Please read Luke 15: 11-31.

What did the younger son request from his father?

How did the younger son use up all his money?

What led the son to come to his senses?

The son then devised a plan to return to his father's house and request to be a servant. Once he had established his plan, what actions did the son take (v. 20)?

What did the father do when he saw his son coming home?

What was the first thing the son said to his father?

This parable answers the question, "What should I do if I have wandered away from God?" The answer is, start walking in the direction back home. This prodigal son stopped his sinful ways, turned around, and started back down the road to redemption. Did you notice the father's response? He didn't wait for his son to reach the doorstep or walk down the road to meet him, He ran with all the strength he had in him. The image of that grown man running toward his son gets me every time. The son did not stop with simply returning home though. The son had an attitude of humility. The first words out of his mouth were to repent for his actions and seek forgiveness.

The parable does not end there. There was still another lesson for us to learn. Upon his son's return, what did the father do next?

Week 2: Centered and Connected

> What was the older brother's response upon hearing the celebration?

If we are honest with ourselves, how many of us have agreed with the older brother? We all want to feel important. Doesn't it seem like the good kids always get overlooked? This brother had remained faithful and was probably doing all the chores of the younger brother in his absence. Where was the acknowledgment and celebration for that service?

Since I am the oldest, I sympathized with the older brother. The sin of self-righteousness creeps up so subtly. I don't think it is possible to fully understand the story of the prodigal son unless you have had to walk the humiliating road back home or walked it with someone. Even though the younger son was welcomed back to the family, I'm sure he carried with him several consequences from his season of wild living. Having to face the ones you love the most and admit your weaknesses and failings, breaks a person. Neither son had the ability to be righteous on their own. The younger son was just more willing to see and admit his shortcomings.

> This question isn't for the group or for you to write down. Which areas of self-righteousness have you been blinded to in your own life? If the Holy Spirit brings something to mind, repent and seek forgiveness.

> What was the father's response to the older brother (V. 31 and 32)?

> Please read Luke 15:1-7. How is verse 7 similar to the father's response to the older son?

If we think that God is not rejoicing over us, we have missed the point of these parables. Our place in the Kingdom is secure. Everything God has is already ours. Once you have the whole inheritance there is nothing more you could possibly have. While God rejoices when a person who was once lost returns to Him, it does not mean He rejoices any less over those who are already His. The banquet God is preparing is for His bride; it is for you.

Having a love for the lost is a supernatural thing and can only happen through the enablement of the Holy Spirit. If you feel a numbness or a disconnect from those who are lost, pray to God for a spirit of mercy and understanding. He will give you eyes to see.

We are all precious and valuable to God. There is no better way to recenter our lives than to start walking home. God will run and meet you where you are.

Week 3
Air Bubbles

Day 1
Armed for Battle

Day 2
Heart to Share

Day 3
Prepared to Share

Day 4
Constant Conversation

Day 5
Train up the Children

Though we have all sinned, God has made a way for our forgiveness. Satan will continue to try to attack believers and leave us ineffective in ministry. God has not left us unprotected. We need to learn to use the tools He has given us. Once we have put on our protective armor, it is time to rescue others in need of salvation. There are simple methods that all of us can use that will enable us to be prepared to share the Good News. The harvest awaits!

Session 3: Viewer Guide
Air Bubbles

Defining Sin

1. Sin is anything we _____, _____, or _____ that displeases God (Matthew 5:21-22).

2. _____ have sinned (Romans 3:23).

Effects of Sin

1. _____ is the only _____ for sin (Romans 6:23).

2. New _____ is required to enter the _____ ___ _____ (John 3:3).

Addressing Sin

1. _____ + _____ ___ _____ = forgiveness of sins (Acts 3:19, 2:38, 26:20).

2. _____ is the _____ _____ to God (John 14:6).

3. _____ + _____ = salvation (Romans 10:9-10).

Salvation and Sanctification

1. Through _____ we are a new _____ (2 Corinthians 5:17).

2. God will continue to _____ us until _____ returns (Philippians 1:6).

Sin After Salvation

1. Our _____ to sin is the same _____ and _____ our salvation.
2. God desires that we would _____ with our sin _____ (Matthew 5:23-24).
3. Do _____ ___ _____ to deal with your sin (Matthew 18:7-9).
4. _____ sin gives Satan a _____ (Ephesians 4:25-27).

Video discussion questions

1. What are some examples of cutting off sin in your life? Why did that particular thing have to be removed? What were the results?
2. How do we give Satan an opportunity by sinning?
3. Is it possible to cause someone else to sin? What does Matthew 18:5-7 have to say about this?
4. Have you ever encountered a question from an unbeliever about sin that you were unable to answer? What was it? Help each other search the Bible for a response.
5. In what areas have you seen God change your life from before you were saved?
6. In what ways can you learn about a potter from looking at the things the potter constructs? In the same way, what can we learn from God as He transforms and changes lives of sinful people?
7. What are some areas where God is still working at refining and "taking out air bubbles" in your life?

Videos are available for viewing at www.jennykaluza.com/the-potter-and-the-clay-videos.

Week 3: Air Bubbles

Day 1
Armed for Battle

In our last session, I outlined verses that clearly stated we are all sinners in need of a Savior. Once we have put our trust in the Lord, Satan still tries to keep us ineffective in our Christian lives. Since he can't have us for keeps, he schemes to trap us and keep us like prisoners even though we are now free. God is aware of the devil's ways and He has equipped each believer with the tools to stand firm against his schemes. Today we will learn what those tools are and how we can put them to use. Please read Ephesians 6:10-18.

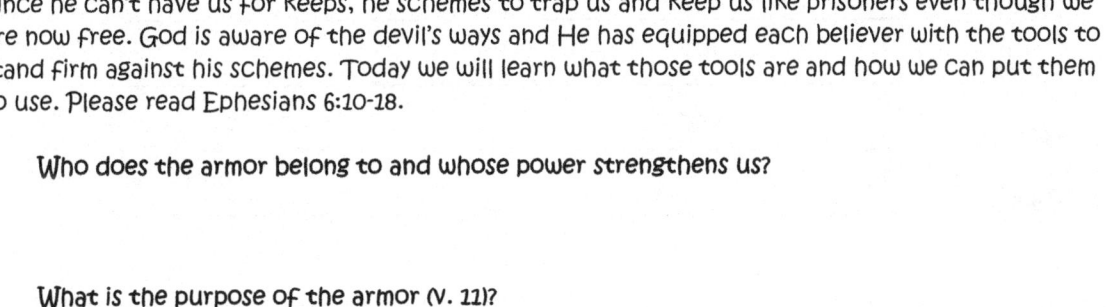

Who does the armor belong to and whose power strengthens us?

What is the purpose of the armor (v. 11)?

Who is our battle against (v.12)?

Both verses 11 and 13 repeat a command telling us to do something. What is it?

So even though we are the ones wearing the armor, the armor does not belong to us. This is an important fact to remember. Apart from God, we can do nothing (John 15:5). Did you notice that the armor enables us to take our stand against Satan? The armor is not so we can wage war against Satan. That is not our job. Our job is to stand firm, and God will fight the battle. The original Greek word for "stand" is *histemi*. It means "to stand, stand immovable, stand firm, stand ready or prepared, to be of a steadfast mind, and the quality of one who does not waiver."[1] No part of the definition has an attacking nature but rather a resoluteness. This resoluteness is important since the armor is not placed on us. We are required to put it on ourselves.

Our battle is not against other humans as much as we can be distracted by dissension and disunity. The battle is being waged in the heavenly realms against an unseen adversary. Therefore, our armor needs to be spiritual in nature. We are going to look at each piece of armor and how it strengthens us. We will also get an idea of what some of the tactics are that the devil might be using to attack us. I will list all of the armor pieces we have been given, and then you may answer which adjective describes the armor and what the opposite of that adjective might be. If God is giving us something for protection it must be protecting us from something. Whatever the opposite of the armor is will most likely be a scheme the devil is using to make us unsteady.

	Adjective	Antonym
Belt	_____	_____
Breastplate	_____	_____
Shoes	_____	_____
Shield	_____	_____
Helmet	_____	_____
Sword	_____	_____

God has given us all of these pieces of armor for a purpose. If all of Satan's attacks were blatant and obvious it would be easy to avoid the snares. We need to know the truth so we can recognize the lies. We need to live righteously so no fault can be found in our integrity which so often happens with unrighteous living. Righteous living assures that no accusations can be made against us. We need to understand the gospel which gives peace so our lives are not characterized by strife. We need a strong faith so we can extinguish the doubts. We need the expectant hope of our salvation so we are safe both now and for eternity. And finally, we need the sword of the Spirit which is the Word of God. This final piece of armor is not really armor at all but rather our only offensive weapon. The Word of God can be used to defend against Satan's attacks but it is also used offensively.

Please read Matthew 4:1-11. How did Jesus use the Word of God when tempted by the devil?

The devil tried many ways to tempt Jesus. He even used the Scripture to try and get Jesus to test God. Each time, Jesus quoted Scripture and the devil's schemes were rendered useless. We need to know the Word. Not only do we need to have a clear understanding, but we need to meditate on it so it is impressed upon our hearts. You may not have time to thumb through a concordance the next time Satan comes at you with a trap.

What is the last thing we need to do so we can stand firm (v. 18)?

Prayer is so often overlooked. Do you hear the urgency in this verse? Pray at all times, in all ways, keep praying! I know God has kept the heavenly realm unseen to us for a reason. Perhaps we couldn't handle the reality of it all. The glimpses we do get on this earth should be enough reason to keep us praying without ceasing. Do not let the reality of these verses cause you to fear. Remember it is not our armor or our power! We don't need anything more than what God has already given us. We just have to remember to put it on!

Week 3: Air Bubbles

Day 2
Heart to Share

Sharing your faith with those you love can be a scary thing. Often we do not feel equipped enough in our understanding of the Scriptures. So rather than sharing the little we know, we avoid the topic altogether. For the remainder of this week, we are going to learn easy ways to use the knowledge we have to greatly impact our world.

Take some time and think about what fears you have in sharing your faith and why you have not shared in the past. In the book *Share Jesus Without Fear* by William Fay, he shares a startling statistic, "Only 10 percent of any church congregation, regardless of the denomination, has shared their faith in the last year."[2]

> What has kept you from sharing your faith in the past? What are your fears?

I have worked for many amazing Christian ministries and attended evangelism training many times. I have stood on the street corner passing out soda pop to strangers and sharing the hope of Jesus' life to anyone who would listen. I have participated in free work projects throughout the neighborhoods of our city in an attempt to share the love of Jesus. All of these public acts are still easier than sitting down with my neighbor or trying to share with my family. Easier still is when I went on a mission trip to Costa Rica and shared with strangers in another language. Why is that? For me, I know I am still working through my desire to receive praise from man rather than praise from God. I fear looking like a fool and sounding unintelligent. I fear people's opinions and losing friendships. I fear further separating myself from family I so dearly love. When I write it all down it sounds kind of ridiculous. The people I love the most are the people I am the least likely to share with. How can we get over our fear? I think it comes down to a battle of the wills. Please read Matthew 28:18-20.

> What did Jesus tell His disciples to do? Was it a command or a suggestion? Does this verse apply to present day disciples?

> Please read James 4:17. What is considered sin in this verse?

> Please read Mark 8:34-38. If we are ashamed of Jesus what is the result (v.38)?

I think the first step in getting over our fear is deciding if we are going to be obedient or not. Jesus clearly stated His desire for His disciples was to share the Gospel. If we know the truth and choose not to do it, we are sinning. When we choose to follow Christ, we are choosing to deny this life. Look back at verse 38 in Mark where it says if we are ashamed of Christ He will be ashamed of us when He returns. This type of shame is a denial of Christ and an act of placing your allegiance in this world. This does not mean that if you have been embarrassed to share your faith with a friend that you will no longer be welcomed in Heaven. It is, however, a reminder to us all that the opinions of a sinful world should not keep us from being bold in our faith. Our goal is to be unashamed.

There is another wonderful outcome when we share our faith. Please read Philemon 6.

> **What positive result happens when we share our faith?**

The more you share your faith, the more you realize all the wonderful things you have been blessed with in Christ. By sharing with others, we are also reminding ourselves. I think this is another key to how we get over our fears. Practice! The more you put yourself out there, the easier it becomes.

The first step in evangelizing is to choose obedience to God. The next step is to be prepared.

> **Please read 1 Peter 3:15-16. When should we be prepared and how should we do it?**

I think there are two key ways that we are prepared. The first is through prayer and the second is through the power of the Holy Spirit. We must have a love for the lost and a burden for the harvest before we share our faith. We must care about the people we are witnessing to. These are all things we can and should be praying for. We will never be eloquent or prepared enough to share our faith in our own power. We can never change the heart of a lost person. It is only by the power of the Holy Spirit that change happens.

> **Please read Matthew 9:37-38 and 1 Corinthians 9:19-23. How do these verses express a love for the lost?**

> **Please read Acts 1:8 and 1 Corinthians 2:1-5. Why do we need the Holy Spirit?**

We need to be mindful of who we are talking to when we share our faith. We don't have to become someone else, but we will be most effective when witnessing if we show an understanding of where the other person is coming from. We need to be able to relate and adapt our style so we draw others near, not push them away. We will never be wise enough, powerful enough, or persuasive enough to affect a life for eternity, but we know Someone who is. Learning to witness is really just learning to rely on the power of the Holy Spirit and being willing to obey His leading.

Week 3: Air Bubbles

Day 3
Prepared to Share

I never get tired of hearing how God has changed a person's life. Each story is so unique, personal, and wonderful. Every time I am at an event and there is an altar call, I can't help but cry just imagining each person's story and how his or her journey is really just beginning. Today we get to take a trip down memory lane and revisit our own story. Think back to the moment when you first believed in Jesus and put your faith in Him.

Who shared their knowledge of Jesus with you? What words did they say?

How would you rate your knowledge of Scripture at the point of your conversion?

If you are like most people, your knowledge of Scripture when you first placed your faith in Jesus was probably very limited compared to where it is now. The person who shared with you was probably not a Greek scholar who had to argue the truths of Scripture to convince you to believe. When the Holy Spirit has enlightened a person's soul, it takes very little convincing for their faith to follow. Why then do we think others need more convincing than what we needed ourselves? I think it is because we so quickly forget that the power does not come from us but from the Holy Spirit. When I look at the ministry of Jesus, I do not see Him chasing after people and spending hours trying to convince them of their need for salvation. Jesus presented the truth. Those whose hearts had already been prepared by the Holy Spirit were ready and followed after Him desperate to hear more. The faster we learn that we have no control over someone else's salvation, the more effective we will be in our witnessing.

All that being said, I can almost feel you all breathing down my neck eager for a specific method that will make sharing your faith a snap. There are several methods that I have been trained in, and there are many useful tools that can increase your confidence. However, I think the most effective tool I can give you is to give you confidence in the knowledge that you already possess, and perhaps show you an easier way to organize some Scriptures. This does not mean you can't also use a particular method if that makes you feel more comfortable. Your local Christian bookstore will be a great resource if you want to dive into that further.

What I want to share with you today is what you can do if someone comes to you wanting to know what they must do to be saved, or if they are having doubts about whether or not they are saved. This is foundational information that I think every Christian needs to know for themselves and be able to teach it. There are three main areas that you will need to address. First, what is the need? Why do we need forgiveness? What is our current state without Christ? Next, who made the way for us to have forgiveness? What actions brought about our reconciliation with God? Finally, how do we receive God's free gift of salvation? What must we do to be saved?

Now that we know the three areas that we must address, the next step is to pick out Scriptures that best explain those questions. There are many Scriptures that address each area. You do not need to know all of them. In fact, if you shared all of them with your listener you would likely lose their attention quickly. It is best to pick out two that you completely understand and have another one as a back-up in case your listener needs the information stated in a different way.

    The following verses all represent the need we all have for a Savior. Read through them all and pick out the two that you understand the best. Isaiah 53:6, John 3:3, Romans 3:23, Romans 5:12, Romans 6:23, and Hebrews 9:27.

    The next verses represent the way we receive forgiveness. Read through them all and pick out the two that you understand the best. John 14:6, Romans 5:8, Ephesians 2:8-9, Titus 3:5, and 1 Peter 3:18.

    Finally these last verses represent what a person must do to receive Christ. Read through them all and pick out the two that you understand the best. John 1:12, John 3:16, John 5:24, Acts 3:19, Romans 10:9-11, and Revelation 3:20.

Ladies I know that was a lot of reading, but it will be worth it. So now that you have six verses picked out, what should you do with them? Memorize them! I think it is great to have the person you are sharing with read the verses for themselves out of a Bible, but that is not always a feasible situation. If you have these verses memorized, you can share anywhere. Make sure you understand the significance of these verses and that you can explain them to someone completely unfamiliar with the Bible. Your notes from our last video session can be helpful with this.

What do you do if the person you are sharing with wants to commit their life to Christ? I would first check for understanding. See if they can explain what you just shared back to you. I think it is a good practice to pray with the person, helping them to confess their need for Jesus, asking for forgiveness, and committing their life to following Him. If you noticed, none of the verses said there was a magic prayer that gets us into Heaven. The key is faith and belief in Jesus. The prayer just helps them to talk to God.

If someone is unsure of their faith or their salvation, I think a good place to start is going back to the basics and making sure they know what they need to do to be saved. If they have already made a commitment to Christ, what they may need to hear are some verses on the assurance of their salvation. Here are some verses that might help: John 5:24, Romans 5:1, Romans 8:1, Romans 8:38-39, and 1 John 5:13. It is crucial to be part of a body of believers. Please help these young Christians get connected to a church where they will be discipled and nurtured. Oh, I can't wait to see how God is going to use you!

Day 4
Constant Conversation

Many of you may be surprised to learn that I am an introvert. I am very comfortable in crowds and can drum up a conversation with just about anyone, but what I love the most is sitting down with a dear friend and chatting over a cup of coffee. There are those with the gift of evangelism that can easily go up to strangers and share their faith. For the rest of us, that thought is terrifying. How you share your faith will depend on your personality. Though the avenues may be different, we all still need to be sharing our faith. I hope to give you some ideas today that will make sharing your faith part of your everyday life and feel natural even if you tend to be shy. Please read 1 Peter 3:15.

Witnessing is both living the Christian life day by day and sharing the Gospel. How we live our lives will cause curiosity but will not provide all the answers. We must also be prepared to give the reason for our hope. The best tool we have for sharing our faith is to learn how to effectively share our lives. People who tend to start arguments over the Scriptures will not be able to argue about the changes that have happened in your life. Having a prepared testimony can be very useful in everyday conversations.

Those of you that accepted Christ into your hearts at a very young age may feel that your testimony is not dramatic enough to share. Every testimony has value and gives glory to God. You may not have a lot to compare with what your life looked like before you were saved, but you have a treasure of examples of how having faith from a young age saved you from many bad decisions that others went through. You may also have walked away from your faith and then had to reconcile with Christ. All of these stories have value.

If we have thought through our testimony and organized it in a way that makes it easy to share, we are more likely to use it. Today I want you to write down your story by answering three questions. Depending on your life, some of your answers to the questions may have more details than others. Practice sharing your story out loud and try to keep it no longer than five minutes. Be mindful of how many details you are giving and how graphic your story is. The goal is to show the amazing difference Christ has made in your life, not how awful of a sinner you were. Please write your answers to the following three questions. If you need more room, please write it on a separate piece of paper.

What was your life like before you met Christ?

What led to your decision to become a Christian?

What difference has Christ made in your life?

The key to being able to share your testimony is listening for the right opportunities. If your conversations are purposeful, you will know when the moments are right. Very rarely will someone just walk up to you and ask to hear your testimony. However, there will be many opportunities when someone will be sharing their pain with you, and you can relate to them by sharing how Christ has helped you in your struggles. There is one final question that will help you prepare to share. Please write down your answer to the following question:

What is God doing in your life right now?

The question that you have just answered is the one that will most often come up in everyday conversation. Everyday conversations can be turned to spiritual conversations by adjusting your testimony to fit the matter at hand. Is the conversation about fear, purity (relationships), unrest, or death? How can you bring elements of your walk with Christ into these conversations? Which topics are normally brought up when you talk to your non-believing friends, family, and neighbors? Plan ahead for the next meeting and anticipate flipping the conversation to spiritual matters.

When having a conversation, remember to ask questions. The questions will help you to know where God is already working in their life. The next thing you need to do is listen to them. It is easy to come in with an agenda, but if you are not listening you will miss your opportunity. Listen for moments in the conversation when you can turn the conversation to spiritual matters. A great question to get you started is to ask if they go to church anywhere. Using natural conversation to bring up spiritual topics and questions will lead to greater opportunities for you to present the Gospel.

I know many of you are still fearful but remember you are not alone. Always use prayer as your greatest tool in witnessing. If you are rejected, it is Christ they are rejecting, not you. Practice sharing your five-minute testimony in pairs with women in your Bible study. Practice hypothetical conversations and turn them into spiritual topics. This can change the way you talk to people, but it will take some practice. I guarantee if you look for opportunities to share the Gospel, you will see them all around you. Remember we serve a purposeful God!

Week 3: Air Bubbles

Day 5
Train up the Children

I have a huge passion for youth ministry. Perhaps it is because that is where I received a foundation for my faith. I came in like a sponge and absorbed everything I heard. This is also where I learned how fun it is to be a Christian. Our faith is not boring and lackluster. My first attempts at water skiing, riding a jet ski, camping on an island, playing capture the flag, snowboarding, and acting in a play all happened in youth group. The Christian life is full of adventure!

Youth group is also where I learned to study God's Word for myself and ask questions in a safe environment. I learned the power of prayer and how to worship not only with my voice but with my life. I learned the value of Christian friendships, which was something I had never had before. I was already a passionate person, but this environment fanned the flame.

As I have grown older, I have seen how hard it is to witness to people once the pressures and distractions of life are added. I saw many kids whose faith had not been solidified in youth go off to college and completely abandon God. I do not know what the statistic is for how many people come to a faith in Jesus after college, but I know it is not high. That does not mean it is impossible, but it does mean we should be putting a great emphasis on reaching the children and youth in our lives.

The Scriptures place a great emphasis on a parent's duty to teach their children God's ways. If you are not a parent that does not mean you are off the hook. Please read through these next verses thinking about how you can reach the children in your life or in your church.

> **Please read Ephesians 6:4, Deuteronomy 6:6-9, and Deuteronomy 4:9. What are some examples these verses give for teaching our children?**

There are a couple of things that stand out to me in these verses. I love that Deuteronomy 4:9 emphasized the importance of not forgetting what the Lord has done for us. Our faith needs to remain strong so we can impart our wisdom to the next generation. I also saw two types of teaching represented. One method seemed to be incorporating the lessons of the Scriptures into our everyday lives, and the other seemed to be focused on a more direct instruction method.

> **What are some ways we can teach the Scriptures through everyday interactions with our children? What are some purposeful activities you already do as a family, and what other ideas do you have?**

What are some ways your family teaches directly from the Scriptures? How do you make reading from God's Word enjoyable and understandable to children?

Which method of teaching children comes most naturally to you, everyday conversations or specific times in the Word? How can you strengthen your weak area?

During Jesus' time on Earth He never married or had children, but that did not change His opinion or love for them.

Please read Matthew 18:2-6, Matthew 19:13-14, and Matthew 21:14-16. What was Jesus' overall opinion of children and what value did He place on them?

What lessons can we learn from children?

It is easy to see that Jesus loved children and humbling to see all we can learn from them. I know they are messy little creatures, and you would likely have fewer headaches if you avoid them, but you would also miss out on an amazing treasure.

The Israelites had many traditions that passed down the stories of the amazing feats the Lord had done in their lives. Our culture is greatly lacking in this area. Although it may be easier to only socialize within your age group, a great travesty happens. We fail to learn from each other. Children have much to teach us and so do our elders.

Evangelism is really the same no matter which age group you are speaking to. It is just a matter of finding creative ways to share our lives and God's Word with others. Children have a teachable spirit and an ability to listen that can diminish with age. Take every opportunity you have to share God's love and truth with them while they are still listening. They are precious in His sight!

I hope you are leaving this week just a little more prepared than when you started. God is not looking for wise and persuasive words. He is looking for a humble and obedient heart. "The harvest is plentiful but the workers are few. Ask the Lord of the harvest, therefore, to send out workers into His harvest field" (Matthew 9:37-38).

Week 4
Molded and Shaped

Day 1
Further Still

    Day 2
Diamond in the Rough

        Day 3
A New Thing

            Day 4
Suffering Servant

                Day 5
Responding to Reshaping

This week is when we really get to see the piece take shape. All of our preparation is finished, and it is time for some dramatic changes. Changes are not always easy, and it always moves us beyond our comfort zone. It is time for an adventure. Though it may feel like a runaway train, our Engineer is still at the controls. So how about it, are you ready for a ride?

Session 4: Viewer Guide
Molded and Shaped

Molded and Shaped into Christ's image

The words "mold," "shape," and "conform" are all used interchangeably in the Bible. Vine's Expository Dictionary defines conform as, "to fashion or shape one thing like another. The verb has reference to that which is changeable or unstable to that which is durable or complete."[1]

1. All things are _____ if they transform us into the _____ _____ _____ (Romans 8:28-29).

2. Our _____ _____ will be transformed into _____ _____ (Philippians 3:20-21).

3. You will have to choose what _____ you are following after (1 Peter 1:14-15).

Reshaped for Another Purpose

1. Sovereignty is God's _____ _____ to do all things according to His own _____ _____. (Easton's Bible Dictionary)[2]

2. God's desire is always to _____ us not to make something _____ (Jeremiah 18:1-10).

3. Knowing the _____ of God helps us to trust in His _____.

4. How we _____ to times of reshaping is our greatest _____ to nonbelievers (Philippians 1:12-18).

5. How can you use your times of _____ to advance the _____?

6. God is all about doing a _____ _____ (Isaiah 43:19).

Video discussion questions

1. What new insights did you gain from Vine's Dictionary definition of the word "conform"? What about the word "good" in Romans 8:28. Can you see that in all things God works for the good, or is this concept still difficult to embrace?
2. Does the thought that you can conform to your evil desires cause you concern? And what about the solution to be holy in all that you do? Does the thought of being holy overwhelm you? What hope do you have in this area?
3. In Jeremiah 18, the potter reshaped the piece he was working on rather than starting over with a new piece. What does this tell you about God's ways?
4. Has God ever used a hard time in your life to spread the Gospel? Have you ever seen someone suffer well? What impact did this have?
5. What new thing is God doing in your life right now?

Videos are available for viewing at www.jennykaluza.com/the-potter-and-the-clay-videos.

Day 1
Further Still

My favorite part of throwing a pot is when I get to mold and shape it. Some of the preparations that happen at the beginning can feel tedious, and the centering of the piece is extremely physical. Once it gets to the molding and the shaping stage all my creativity can flow, and there is this beautiful rhythm of moving with the piece. This stage is also extremely challenging due to the amount of focus the potter must have. If the walls are left too thick, the piece will be heavy and its usefulness limited. If the walls are stretched too thin, the piece will not be able to hold its shape and will collapse. The potter's job is to know the limitations of the clay while at the same time stretching it as far as possible so all of its beautiful qualities can be displayed. This is when the shape and character of the piece are seen for the first time.

You will know when you are going through a season of being molded and shaped by God when you are stretched beyond the abilities that you currently possess. God never wants us to get too comfortable. When we are comfortable we stop growing, and we can easily forget that we need the power of God. I am so thankful God included some stories in the Bible that allow us to see large portions of a person's. This helps us to see how He applied that molding and shaping process.

The book of Esther takes place during the Persian rule. Israel had already been allowed to return to their homeland and rebuild the temple after a time of captivity in Babylon. Several Israelites chose not to return to their homeland and instead lived amongst the Persians in a foreign land. King Xerxes was reigning as king, and Queen Vashti was his wife. During a long season of feasting, Queen Vashti refused to be brought before the king's guest for their entertainment and angered the king. The king's advisors recommended that Queen Vashti be banished and a new queen found to replace her. Please read Esther 2:1-18.

> **What details do we know about Esther before she was brought into the king's palace? What do you think her daily life was like?**

> **What was Esther's life like once she was taken to the palace? How long did she receive beauty treatments?**

> **What do you think Esther was feeling and thinking during her year of preparation to meet the king?**

Talk about a life change! We don't know how wealthy Esther was before she was selected to live in the palace, but I certainly don't imagine her eating and receiving beauty treatments all day. Even though this new lifestyle was probably more comfortable than what she was used to, I imagine she

Week 4: Molded and Shaped

had some fears and trepidations. I wonder if there were moments when she just wished to be average. I wonder if she felt forgotten by God and completely out of her element.

Esther was being molded and shaped by God before she even realized it. Even before Israel knew they needed help, God was paving the way. Please read Esther 3:8-9, 4:6-16, and 7:1-4.

What problem arose for the Jews?

What request did Mordecai make of Esther? Why do you think she obeyed him?

Esther was being molded and shaped to be a queen. A decree for annihilation of this magnitude could only come from the king. If there was to be a change, of course, it also had to come from a position of power. God had already shaped obedience into Esther and given her characteristics that quickly found favor with the king. The king could not undo the original decree, but he could write an additional one. The Jews were allowed to defend themselves, and they were victorious in battle. God had once again protected His people. In all those months of preparation, I don't think Esther ever imagined that the transformation God was bringing about in her would one day save a nation.

How have you seen God stretch you beyond your current capabilities?

If my English teachers knew I was writing a Bible study, I'm sure they would have concerns. I am what you call a late bloomer. All through elementary school, I was pulled out of my classes to receive extra help with reading and math. Things took a long time to click for me. Eventually by junior high, math became easy, and I went on to the advanced classes. This was not the case for English. English remained a struggle all through high school. By college my skills were improving, and oddly enough, a linguistics class for Spanish helped me understand English better. I still did not enjoy writing, and my papers would keep me up well into the night. What came easy for others was sheer willpower for me. If you would have told me that one day I would willingly write a paper every day, I would not have believed it.

God has taken my love for His Word and an urgency to share it and paired it with an ability to write. I know this is a God thing because there is no way I would have picked this path on my own. I did not possess these abilities. God stretched me beyond what I could do on my own so that it wouldn't be my skill that was displayed, but His power.

There are so many uncertainties when we are stretched beyond our means. Our instinct is to recoil and return to what is comfortable. It is only when we move in rhythm with the Potter that hidden qualities are revealed. Follow the movements of His hands, for such a time as this!

Day 2
Diamond in the Rough

There are a couple people in my life that I know have not realized their full potential. Part of the reason is that they do not see themselves as capable of anything more. They feel stuck and unable to make any lasting changes. This is the unfortunate result when we are only tapping into limited resources. God's resources are limitless, and only He knows our true potential. God is so focused on the end result that He calls us by our potential, not our current state. Please read Judges 6:1-16.

Why were all the Israelites hiding in caves?

When the angel appeared to Gideon, what did he call him?

When the angel commissioned Gideon to go out and conquer the Midianites, how did Gideon respond?

Why would Gideon be victorious?

In week nine of our study, we will finish the story of Gideon so I will try not to ruin the surprise. Without giving too much away, Israel did defeat the Midianites under Gideon's leadership. God didn't wait until Gideon was victorious in battle to acknowledge his potential. He called him a mighty warrior before Gideon ever realized his abilities, or rather, what his abilities would become when God was with him. I so love that about our God. Whether you can audibly hear it or not, God is already calling you by your potential.

Please read 1 Samuel 16:7. Samuel was at the house of Jesse to appoint the next king for Israel. Why does God have a different perspective than people on a person's worth?

God sees what no one else can see. He knows what circumstances will bring out the character that He desires to develop in us. We tend to judge a book by its cover and set limits on others and ourselves. Throughout the Bible, God specifically picked out people for tasks who didn't seem to possess the right qualities for the job. He did this so that they would not boast in their own achievements but in the power of God.

Week 4: Molded and Shaped

Perhaps the most unlikely group of leaders are the men Jesus gathered to be His twelve apostles. I'm not sure there is any profession that would have trained them for the type of ministry Jesus had for them, but I'm quite sure none of them were prepared for how their lives would change.

>Please read Matthew 4:18-22. Please list the name of each man and what profession they had before following Jesus.

>Please read Luke 5:27-29. What is the name of this apostle and what profession did he have before following Jesus?

>What do you see as some positive characteristics people with these professions might have and what might be some negative characteristics?

At least four of the twelve apostles were fishermen. There could have been several others as well. In John 21:1-3 six disciples go along with Peter on a fishing expedition. That doesn't necessarily mean all were fishermen, but they all were comfortable on a boat. Levi, who is also called Matthew, is the only disciple that we know of who was a tax collector. As for the rest, we are never given their specific profession. None of the apostles were Pharisees, theologians, or scholars of their day. This is the type of profession we might expect. Paul later became an apostle after Jesus' resurrection, and he previously was a Pharisee. It took a supernatural encounter with Jesus to change his life.

When I think about the characteristics of fishermen, I think of down to earth, hard-working, straight-talking men. They most likely started working at a young age to help support their families and probably did not have any formal training as rabbis. After Jesus called these men, they had their share of doubts and failures, but eventually their faith would become so firm that they would be willing to die for it. Often when they spoke from the Scriptures, the crowd was baffled by their knowledge. They spoke with wisdom and authority that would not have come from their profession. Jesus knew what He was doing. Their knowledge of the Scripture had to point to the work of the Holy Spirit in their lives.

Matthew would have been an unlikely pick as well. Tax collectors were generally disliked by the Jews. Their job was to collect taxes from the Jewish people to give to the Roman government. They also got to keep a portion for themselves. They were seen as traitors to their own people. When Jesus called Matthew, he instantly followed and left his former life behind. His inclusion in the group of apostles shows that Jesus came to the earth to save sinners. No one is beyond forgiveness. This was not an exclusive club based on the skills and status of its members. Jesus called this group of men based on the purposes He knew they would later fulfill. Ladies, He is calling you, too. He is calling you as the finished masterpiece He is creating you to be.

Day 3
A New Thing

After college, I lived with three amazing, adventurous, Christian women. We challenged and stretched each other to grow in new ways. We were all very different people, but there was a great harmony in our friendship. One particular afternoon one of the gals got the idea that while our other roommate was at work we should all completely rearrange her room. We all went along with this idea. We completely emptied her room and then put everything back in a completely different arrangement. All of this was done with care so nothing was damaged, but everything was completely rearranged and redecorated when we were done. When our roommate returned home from work, she was thrilled with the new arrangement.

I'm not sure how thrilled I would be if they had chosen my room for the makeover. I am far more likely to arrange my furniture in a way that feels comfortable and then leave it like that for the rest of my life! I usually do not test out a new arrangement unless I move or remodel. I know what I like and change seems unneeded. This is why I need movers and shakers in my life.

God is all about doing new things. If we keep doing things the same old way we will never grow and change. Change is necessary to be conformed into Christ's likeness.

> Please read 2 Corinthians 5:17. What is the result of belonging to Christ?

Instantly Christ starts doing a new thing in us the moment we belong to Him. He doesn't ease us into the new change. The old is gone! The new things that come are not a once and for all change but rather a pattern for the rest of our lives. Change is now the new normal.

> Please read Isaiah 42:9, 43:18-19, 48:6, and 65:17-18. Why do you think God loves doing a new thing?

> What new thing is God doing in your life?

> Why do you think new things can be scary? Can you think of a time when you resisted something new? What were your fears?

New means change, and change means uncertainty. We often like to stay where it is familiar even if the new thing is better. Habits can be comforting but can also lead to stagnancy. We cannot stay in one place in our relationship with Christ. We are either moving toward Him or away from Him. If we

Week 4: Molded and Shaped

are moving toward Christ, more of our self needs to die so that more of Him can be revealed in our life. These new changes He is making in us do not stop until we reach Heaven.

Not only does God like doing a new thing, but He likes hearing a new song. Please read Psalm 33:1-4, 40:1-3, 96:1-3, and Isaiah 42:10-11.

Why is singing a new song to God important?

I had to contain myself to not have you read every verse in the Bible that tells us to sing a new song to our Savior. If God is doing a new thing in your life, you will need new words to express it. I get so tired of what the church refers to as "worship wars." God doesn't care what style we are singing in. He just wants to know that our heart is still being moved by what He is doing in our life.

I did not grow up with hymns. There are many hymns that when I hear them for the first time they are a new song for me. New doesn't necessarily mean current. It is great to sing an old favorite and remember the blessings of the past, but God also wants us to have a new song in our hearts that praise Him for what He is doing right now. I love when I hear a new song on the radio or from the worship team, and I have to just stop and listen. It is not familiar to me so I can't sing along. I am forced to focus on the words and see if they resonate with my heart. And if they do, watch out! I'll start singing whether I have mastered the melody or not.

We are not the only ones singing a new song. Oh, I am so excited! Please read Revelation 5:6-14.

Why were the angels singing a new song?

I cannot wait to hear the praises of the angels! I had to take a moment before I could see my keyboard to type again. This scene in Heaven overwhelms me. A new scene unfolded in Heaven, and the angels needed a new song to go with it.

Please read Revelation 4:8. How long had the angels been singing this previous song?

These creatures were compelled to proclaim the holiness of God night and day without ceasing. Picture this with me, imagine the sounds. Their song was repeated over and over again until the Lamb stretched out His hand to open the scroll. All of a sudden a new song burst forth in Heaven. Imagine the sound of thousands upon thousands of angels singing, "Worthy is the Lamb, who was slain, to receive power and wealth and wisdom and strength and honor and glory and praise!" Ladies, take some time today to thank God for the new things He is doing in your life. Sing to Him a new song of praise!

Day 4
Suffering Servant

So far we have seen that God can mold and shape us through new circumstance and changes in our lives, but we haven't yet talked about the pain that can be involved. The pain involved in being molded and shaped into Christ's likeness can be mental, physical, emotional, and spiritual. Christ also experienced all of these types of pain.

Please read Mark 3:20 and 6:30-31. How do these verses represent physical pain?

I like to joke that Mark must have been hypoglycemic. Only in his gospel do we learn that the ministry of Jesus was so physically demanding that they often were unable to eat. This is just one small detail to what I'm sure were many physical stresses caused by a life on the road. Physical pain is characterized by pain in your body. It can be brought on by stress, injury, illness, or disease.

Describe a time of physical pain in your life. What did God teach you from the pain?

Please read Luke 19:41-42 and John 11:32-36. How do these verses represent emotional pain?

Sometimes we forget that not only is Jesus God, He was also completely human. He loved deeply and shared His emotions with others. He didn't endure pain without showing emotion, as to seem stoic, but was real about His feelings. You can be certain that when you are feeling pain He is sympathizing with you, too. Emotional pain is characterized by overwhelming sadness and grief. It can be exhibited with a large amount of emotion or none at all.

Describe a time of emotional pain in your life. What did God teach you from the pain?

Please read Matthew 4:1-11 and 22:15-18. How do these verses represent mental anguish?

Now we know that Jesus had fasted for forty days and forty nights, but the real struggle here was not physical. I'm sure the physical strain was taking its toll, but Jesus had to keep His wits about Him to defeat the devil. Not all struggles are cut and dry. Any time we are tempted, I think there is also a spiritual battle. The Pharisees loved to test Jesus' mental capabilities and were always trying

Week 4: Molded and Shaped

to catch Him in a trap regarding His interpretations of Scripture. Mental anguish is characterized by anything that impairs your ability to think clearly and reasonably.

Describe a time of mental anguish in your life. What did God teach you from the pain?

Please read Luke 22:39-46. How do these verses represent spiritual pain?

Some people assume that Jesus feared the pain of death in this passage. I don't think it was the physical pain He feared but the burden of bearing the sins of the world and experiencing separation from God the Father. This was a type of pain He had never had to experience before. Spiritual pain is characterized by an attack on your core beliefs. The meaning and purpose of your life may come into question.

Describe a time of spiritual pain in your life. What did God teach you from the pain?

Though Jesus experienced various types of pain throughout His life, the cross represents all types of suffering. Please read Matthew 27:26-50.

Please list out the examples you see of each type of pain.

Physical _____ Emotional _____

Mental _____ Spiritual _____

There are many reasons why Jesus chose not to escape the pains of human life. I know we have read a lot today but I promise these last verses will be worth it. Please read Hebrews 4:14-16 and 12:3.

Why did Jesus endure such great pain?

Jesus sympathizes with us and knows what we are going through. We can go confidently before His throne and ask for help. We can have confidence that there will be an end to our suffering, and God will use our suffering to mold and shape us so we will look more like Jesus day by day. God uses many methods to conform and shape us, but nothing is quite as motivating and effective as pain. I hope you could see how even though you have had seasons of great pain, God was also bringing about a great work in you. If you have yet to see God's hand upon your life, remain faithful and He will continue the good work. His mercy and grace are sufficient.

Day 5
Responding to Reshaping

As a kid, my parents played a lot of contemporary Christian music in the house. There was one particular album by Bebe and Cece Winans that we all liked to dance to due to the upbeat tempo. The first song was titled, "Count it all Joy." This song had a slow start but then really picked up by the end. Who can sit still when the song is singing about joy? Like most Christian songs, I had no idea that the lyrics were actually words from the Scriptures. When I read the words for the first time, they didn't have nearly the same happy tune as the song.

Please read James 1:2-3. What are we to count as pure joy? Why?

Hold on a minute! Did James just tell us to count our trials pure joy? Not our salvation, not Jesus' love for us, but our trials? Trials can't possibly mean what I think it does. Well, in fact, this word "trial" in the Bible can also mean temptation, adversity, affliction, and trouble. Perhaps Bebe and Cece got it wrong. I don't feel much like dancing anymore.

Jesus never forces us to do things. He gives us choices and then the decision is up to us. The word "count" in James 1:2 is translated in other versions of the Bible as "consider." We have a choice in how we are going to respond to the trials in our lives. Our response will also affect others. The original Greek word for "count" is *hegeomai*. When used in other verses of the Bible it means, "leader, to go before, to have authority over, influence, and to think."[3] How we respond to trials sets an example for others and affects their behavior as well.

While I was in college I was required to read the book *Man's Search for Meaning* by Viktor Frankl. In it I found one of my favorite quotes. "We who lived in concentration camps can remember the men who walked through the huts comforting others, giving away their last piece of bread. They may have been few in number, but they offer sufficient proof that everything can be taken from a man but one thing: the last of the human freedoms – to choose one's attitude in any given set of circumstances, to choose one's own way."[4]

We may not have a choice in our circumstances, but we do have a choice in how we respond. It is the responses to those circumstances that I have seen drive people away from God or draw them closer to Him. The people that draw near to God in hard times are the ones who develop perseverance of the faith, and that is certainly something to be joyful about.

I think all of us would like to think we would draw near to God in hardships, but you don't know for sure until you are faced with one. There are three responses that I have seen help people endure their trials resulting in glorifying God and perfecting their faith.

1. The first response is that they are not surprised by their trials. They did not receive a prophetic word about their specific trial, but they knew trials would come in their lifetime. This made it easier for them to not feel picked on or punished by God.

Week 4: Molded and Shaped

> Please read 1 Thessalonians 3:2-4. Why would knowing in advance that trials are coming help you to persevere?

2. The second response is that they remained focused on the outcome their trial would serve. Some people just have a positive nature, but what we are focusing on also influences our outlook. If you are focusing on the pain of suffering, your outlook will be negative. If you are focusing on the glory being revealed, your outlook will be positive.

    > Please read 2 Corinthians 1:3-5, 12:8-10 and James 1:3. What are some positive outcomes that come from seasons of suffering?

3. The third response is that they prayed and those close to them prayed. Going through trials requires endurance and strength that we do not possess in our own abilities. God is the only one who can strengthen us and ensure that our pain is not in vain.

    > Please read Romans 8:26-27. Why is prayer important in a time of weakness?

> Of these three responses, which one is hardest for you? How can you better equip yourself?

Sometimes what are actually choices don't seem like choices at the time. Having to pick between broccoli and green beans may not feel like a choice if you know you will still have to eat your vegetables. To avoid constant emotional meltdowns that often happen between the ages of two and three, we try to give our children small choices involving their daily routine. For example, I will pull out two outfits, and they get to pick which one they like. One of our children quickly caught on to our system of choices and when offered a choice responded, "Neither." Unfortunately for her, not wearing clothes for the day was not an option. Having to pick between joy and resentment may not feel like a choice if you know you will still have to walk through the trial. This is not a lesson on how to avoid trials, but rather how you can respond when faced by one. Trials will come. How you respond has a lasting effect.

If we are just responding out of instinct, allowing the first emotion that presents itself to guide us, we are headed for a frustrating journey. Nothing is more annoying than feeling something is pointless and a waste of time. If you are unable to consider it joy for yourself, maybe you would be willing to draw near to God for someone else's benefit. Have you ever witnessed someone walk with God through a difficult season? How did their faith influence you? Consider how your faith may encourage another sister or brother in Christ. Consider it joy!

Week 5
A Lighter Load

Day 1
Gain the World

Day 2
Out of this World

Day 3
Mind over Matter

Day 4
Heart of the Matter

Day 5
A Way with Words

Trimming is a time consuming task for the potter. I often joke with my husband that I am going to teach him how to trim so I can just do the fun parts of pottery. I don't particularly like to trim a piece since there is not a lot of creativity involved. It takes just as much time to trim a piece as it does to form it. The goal of trimming is to remove the excess weight of the piece so it can function best for the purposes I am creating it for. Before I can get back to the creative work of decorating and designing the piece, I have to prepare the piece through trimming. I continue to trim my pieces even though it is not my favorite part because I want my pieces to reach their full potential. This week we will look at areas in our lives where we tend to keep some extra weight and discover solutions to remove the weight.

Session 5: Viewer Guide
A Lighter Load

A Trimmed Pot

God is not satisfied with "good enough." He has given us tools to trim off things that are weighing us down so we might be useful to Him. (2 Timothy 2:19-22)

1. Trim off _____ and _____ (vs. 19, 22).

2. Pursue _____, _____, _____, and _____. (vs. 22)

3. We will be an instrument for _____ _____, made _____, _____ to the Master and prepared to do _____ _____ work (vs. 21).

Burden is Light

There are two types of yokes.

1. The yoke of the world. Isaiah 14:25, Nahum 1:13, Leviticus 26:13, Deuteronomy 28:47-48, Isaiah 58:9-10, and Lamentations 1:14.

   A. The words that describe the yoke of the world are _____, _____, _____, _____, _____, _____, _____, and _____.

   B. _____ is the image that is described.

   C. The yoke of the world is the _____ _____ _____ (Proverbs 5:22, Hebrews 12:1).

2. The yoke of Christ. Ezekiel 34:27, Hosea 11:4, Galatians 5:1, and Matthew 11:28-30.

   A. The words that describe the yoke of Christ are _____, _____, _____, _____, _____, _____, _____, and _____.

   B. _____ is the yoke of Christ (Luke 11:28, John 14:23, John 15:10, 1 John 5:3).

Video discussion questions

1. When are we useful to the Master? Do you think it is easier to prepare for God to use you or to prepare for a specific task?
2. Why do you think God likes us to strive for generic things like holiness and righteousness rather than a specific goal?
3. Our temptation is to hide our extra weight, our areas of sin. How does this thinking eventually backfire?
4. Which description of the yoke of the world hit a chord with you? What about the yoke of Christ?
5. Which situations usually lead you to feel burdened by your load? What makes your load feel lighter?
6. Why do you think obedience is such an unpopular topic?
7. In what ways has our American upbringing shaped our view of freedom? What would be a better description of Biblical freedom?

Videos are available for viewing at www.jennykaluza.com/the-potter-and-the-clay-videos.

Day 1
Gain the World

Christmas and New Year's were not that long ago, and now we are being bombarded by all the fitness ads. There is a reason that fitness draws a lot of attention in January and February, and it's not just because of all the new resolutions. We are all feeling a little heavier this time of year due to the overindulgence of the holidays. Imagine now how you would feel if you gained the whole world.

Please read Matthew 16:26. What are some results of gaining the whole world?

Every time we add something we lose something too. It is impossible to hold on to it all. The characteristics of the world are in complete opposition to the characteristics of God, making it impossible to serve both simultaneously. Please read the following verses, and next to each verse list the characteristics of the world or the results of following after the world.

Matthew 18:7 _____

Colossians 2:18 _____

Colossians 3:5-6 _____

James 4:4 _____

1 John 2:15-16 _____

Yuck! Now that is a heavy weight. It is easy to see that God would be opposed to all of those characteristics, but what if we wanted to hold on to something a little less severe? Could we keep our worldly humor or gossip and still walk in the light? We like to put a rating system on our sins so we feel better about the ones we deem less evil, but God has an entirely different rating system. 2 Corinthians 6:14 states, "Do not be yoked together with unbelievers. For what do righteousness and wickedness have in common? Or what fellowship can light have with darkness?" 1 John 1:5 states, "This is the message we have heard from him and declare to you: God is light; in him there is no darkness at all."

Is it possible to be just a little bit bad or keep just a little sin? Why or why not?

It is either light or darkness. There is no gray when it comes to sin. It is either completely righteous and therefore stemming from God, or it is completely wicked and therefore stemming from the world. If God made the world, why is it associated with wickedness? It is not a matter of who created it but rather who is ruling over it.

Please read John 12:31, 2 Corinthians 4:4, Ephesians 2:1-3, 1 John 5:19 and Revelation 12:9. Who is the leader or prince of this world?

What effect does his leadership have on the world?

Please read Luke 4:5-6. How did Satan get control of the Earth?

Satan was not powerful enough to take anything from God. He was given authority on the Earth for a limited time and for a limited purpose. When that purpose is fulfilled, Christ will return and claim what belongs to Him. No authority exists except that which God has established (Romans 13:1). It all comes back to God's sovereignty. The ways of the world will lead toward wickedness because Satan has taken up temporary residence here.

To avoid gaining the whole world we need to trim off anything that resembles the world in our lives. Living a life of righteousness is a battle. It is not a battle we are familiar with fighting so we need to learn new tactics. We need a different battle plan because we are waging a different kind of battle.

Ladies, I know you have followed me all throughout the Scriptures today so I will list out the final three for you here. Ephesians 6:12 states, "For our struggle is not against flesh and blood, but against the rulers, against the authorities, against the powers of this dark world and against the spiritual forces of evil in the heavenly realms." Romans 13:12 states, "The night is nearly over; the day is almost here. So let us put aside the deeds of darkness and put on the armor of light." And finally, 2 Corinthians 10:2-4 states, "I beg you that when I come I may not have to be as bold as I expect to be toward some people who think that we live by the standards of this world. For though we live in the world, we do not wage war as the world does. The weapons we fight with are not the weapons of the world. On the contrary, they have divine power to demolish strongholds."

If we are losing the weight of the world we need to put on something in its place. As easy as it would be to escape to Heaven once we are saved, Christ has a plan for us on this Earth. The ways of the world are tricky and deceiving. We will need the power of God to remain in this world and still be effective. The remainder of this week we will study which tools God has left for us as we remain in this world. Every time we remove an area of sin we will fill it with truth from God. Who is ready for a little heavenly gym time?

Day 2
Out of this World

Life can seem pretty simple and straightforward until you have children. Everyone always tells a pregnant woman, "Your life will never be the same." I assumed they were only speaking of the sleepless nights and busy schedule. I could not possibly grasp the emotional and mental toll children would take on my life. Most people have heard Proverbs 22:6, "Train up a child in the way he should go, and when he is old he will not depart from it." I cannot tell you how many times I have wished there were more specifics to go along with this verse. There are so many options when parenting and many of them seem good at the time. How do we know if the way we are molding our children will lead them to be lifelong followers of Christ?

One of the things my husband and I have struggled with is how we can raise our children to be in the world and not of it. What does that phrase even mean, and where does it come from?

Please read John 17:6-19. Who was Jesus praying for in these verses?

Where was Jesus going and where would His disciples be (v. 11)?

What request did Jesus make of God regarding His disciples in verse 11 and 15?

By what power would they be protected (v.11)?

Why were they hated by the world (v.14)?

What other request did Jesus make on their behalf (v.17)? Why would they need that?

Why was Jesus sending them into the world?

Jesus did not want his followers to be taken out of the world but rather wanted them protected and sanctified so they could be witnesses of His truth in a dangerous world. After Jesus' death and resurrection, a time of severe persecution would come to the new believers in Christ. Satan did not want the church to be built up. God's plan would prevail, and He would protect them so Christ's message would persevere. They had to remain in meaningful contact with people to spread Christ's message.

Why do you think Christians remain on this Earth after they have been saved?

In what ways are you in the world and not of it? Where could you improve?

It is hard to know how to be in the world but not conformed by it. There are several well-meaning people that set out to share God's truth in the world but instead end up looking just like the world. The other response to the evil in the world is to escape from it. I don't know how many times I have had a conversation in a church setting and the person I am speaking with admits that they have absolutely no one in their life that is not saved. That is completely missing the point of why we are all still here. I love a good night of fellowshipping, but if that is all we are here for, I would much rather hang out with you all in Heaven. There has to be another option for how we can share God's truths with a hurting world and not be led astray ourselves.

Well if we are going out into the world we are going to need a new wardrobe! Please read Romans 13:14, Colossians 3:12, and 1 Peter 5:5.

Please list everything these verses ask you to clothe yourselves in.

Everyone feels better in a new outfit. This new wardrobe also leads to a new identity. We have to intentionally remember the things we are putting on so we are prepared to go out into a world that delights in evil. If you are clothed in Christ and His qualities, you will be renewed and strengthened for the task. Please read Colossians 2:6-7, 2 Peter 1:3-4, and 1 John 4:4.

What strengthens us for life on this Earth?

Don't you see? It's is all about Jesus. If we are clothed in Him, walk in Him, and strengthened by Him, we will persevere with the tasks He has for us. He has given us everything we need. The Victor is on our side. Let Him go into battle ahead of you, and you are guaranteed the victory. He would not leave us here unprotected and without cause. If He didn't have a greater plan in motion, Jesus would want to be beside you now. We are not of this world, but for the time being, we are in it. Choose then to walk by faith. "All these people were still living by faith when they died. They did not receive the things promised; they only saw them and welcomed them from a distance. And they admitted that they were aliens and strangers on earth" (Hebrews 11:13).

Week 5: A Lighter Load

Day 3
Mind over Matter

I love a movie with a good courtroom drama or a mystery to solve. I like to try and figure out who is guilty and what the plot is before it is revealed. I have to be careful though; sometimes these shows can be gory, dark, and scary. I like to think I am unaffected and fine. I'm determined to put on a brave face. All that bravery disappears while I am sleeping though. Suddenly thoughts I thought were under control are now reigning supreme. I have had to stop watching some shows just so I could get a good night's sleep.

The mind is a tricky thing. It absorbs thoughts and ideas without us even being conscious of it. A simple change in radio stations can bring about entirely different feelings, attitudes, and language. The same thing can be said about the people we spend time with. The negative things we are putting into our minds either purposefully or accidentally have negative consequences. Please read each verse listed below, and next to it write the negative thought that can be in our mind.

Luke 1:51 _____   Luke 12:22 _____

Luke 24:37-39 _____   Romans 8:5 _____

Philippians 4:6 _____   1 John 4:18 _____

This list is certainly not meant to be comprehensive, but I think we would all agree these are all thoughts that need to be removed if we are going to have the thoughts of Christ dominating our mind. These thoughts also tend to be sneaky. They all may not seem blatantly evil but that is exactly why we need to be so careful. Worry, doubt, and fear all point to the bigger problem of not trusting in God. If we do not believe and trust God, that is sin. Our thought life can be opposed to the ways of God whether it is intentional or not.

So hopefully we are all in agreement that there are some thoughts that need to be removed from our mind. The idea of clearing your mind so you will be walking around with an empty head is a silly notion. We don't want to simply remove the negative and evil thoughts, we also want to fill our mind with good things. So what are some practical steps we can take to change our thought life?

   Please read Romans 12:2-3. Why do we need to renew our minds?

   Why is it important to have an accurate view of yourself?

The mind is the control center for the rest of your body. If you renew your mind, the rest will follow. God wants us to use our minds. If our minds are functioning properly, we will be able to test and judge what is God's will. We will know what is right. It is easy to get an inflated view of ourselves or see ourselves as less than we are. It is only with sound judgment that we can view ourselves correctly. Though we are intelligent thinking beings, we also need the wisdom of God to guide us. This is a lifelong process. The Greek word used for "transformed" is a present passive imperative, which means the action continues in the future.[1] In other words, we need to keep on being transformed. We never master our thought life. It is only through constant submission to God's work in our lives that we can be renewed. What should you do if an ungodly thought enters your mind?

Please read 2 Corinthians 10:5. What does it mean to take every thought captive?

God's Word is the standard of truth. There has to be a standard to compare things to. God's Word is the standard we use to know if something is a truth or a lie. When a thought enters our mind, we need to grab hold of it and hold it up against the light of God's Word. Both the ideas of renewing your mind and taking your thoughts captive require action. Our thought life cannot be a passive process if we are going to have the victory.

If we are removing the thoughts in our mind that do not align with God's Word, we need to be filling our mind up with replacement thoughts. We battle the lies by replacing them with truth. What is the area in your life that you have been struggling with? Are you feeling like you don't matter? What does God's Word say? Are you anxious and worried? What does God's Word say? Are you spreading gossip? What does God's Word say? Please read Philippians 4:8 and Romans 8:5.

List out all the things we should think about.

Here we get a couple more action words regarding our thoughts. There is a beautiful result if we are purposeful with what we are thinking about and setting our minds on the things of God.

Please read Isaiah 26:3. What is the result of having a mind fixed on Jesus?

I don't know about you, but I could use a little perfect peace. This world we live in both assaults our thought life and deceptively desensitizes us to the things of this world. We have to be actively engaging our minds to take every thought captive. I once had a pastor that made a very poignant word picture of this idea. He held up a glass of Pepsi and a little crumb of a Cheerio. He asked the group to imagine the tiny piece of Cheerio was poop and then proceeded to drop it in the glass. He then asked us if we would still drink the Pepsi. Of course, no one would. That one little piece ruined the entire drink. That is exactly what we face every day. There are hidden lies and messages in everything we watch and listen to. Does your thought life pass the Philippians 4:8 test? It might be time for some renewal.

Day 4
Heart of the Matter

My sister, Anna, is the most tenderhearted person I know. I come from a long line of tenderhearted people, but she takes the cake. Zach and I wanted to get a new cat from our local animal shelter. I took Anna and another sister, Dani, to go and pick out our new pet. I was to find a female short-haired cat. The three of us split up in our search to find the perfect cat. There was one cat that kept sticking his paws out of his cage in an attempt to lure you close. I went over to look at him, but he was in bad shape. His legs were shaved because of multiple cuts, and he had been recently neutered so his long hair was matted and greasy. There was no way I was going near that cat. Dani and I continued to roam the room, but Anna was lured in by this homely cat. She got him out of the cage and held him for the rest of the time. One of the employees came into the room, and I asked her what her favorite cat was. She pointed to the one Anna was holding. I politely asked her what her second favorite was. I proceeded to go and play with her second choice but did not feel any special bond. Finally, I went back to the homely cat still in Anna's arms. I picked up the cat, and he instantly put his paw on my face. The next thing I know I'm calling Zach begging him to accept this long-haired male cat into our home. Let's just say this man loves his wife, and "Bug" has been a permanent member of our family for the last ten years.

What is in a person's heart tells you a lot about them. The mind might be the body's control center, but the heart is where all the passions and emotions lie. Our passions are a window into what our heart follows after. If controlled by the Spirit, they inspire and accomplish great things in the name of Jesus. If controlled by selfish desires, our passions damage and hurt others.

Please read Genesis 8:21. What is the nature of the heart?

Please read Matthew 15:18-19 and Mark 7:21-23. Please list every sin mentioned that comes from the heart.

Why do you think those sins are attributed with the heart?

Just as we all have a sin nature since the fall of Adam and Eve, so the nature of our heart is also evil. The sins of the heart are often not calculated and well thought out. They are what the world refers to as crimes of passion. Even the most cautious and intelligent people can quickly be led astray by the impulses of the heart. There are several phases in the Bible that attach emotion to the heart; sick in heart, heart cries, agony of heart, anguish of heart, heart yearns, heart laments, heart longs, and heart loves. How can we point all this passion in the right direction? Please read Proverbs 4:23 and Matthew 6:21.

We are familiar with guarding treasure, but why would our heart need guarding?

Please read Deuteronomy 30:14, Romans 10:8-10, 2 Corinthians 1:22, and Ephesians 3:17. Besides passions, what else resides in a believer's heart?

I find it very interesting that the Bible says God's Word resides in our hearts. When I think of books, information, and rules, I think of the mind. God's Word should also be in our mind, but believing in Jesus is not just a religion but a relationship. Your life will never be altered unless Jesus is in your heart. Think of other people you deeply love. Is it an intellectual relationship or a heart relationship? The Holy Spirit and Jesus reside in a believer's heart because He wants to be the one true passion of your life. When you have an undivided heart solely focused on Jesus, the passions and desires of your heart will be His desires as well.

Keeping guard of your passions can be exhausting work. Often people who are seen as the most passionate are also the ones most at risk for depression or burn out at work. Nurses, child-care workers, and social workers are some of the professions with the highest turnover rate. Feeling so deeply every day can take a physical toll on a person. As a protective measure, we build walls around our heart. If you have a calloused heart, it will be difficult to still do those jobs that need passion. Constantly working to obey and love God can also be an emotional drain if you are using your own strength. When people in the Bible stopped listening and obeying God, their hearts became calloused and hard. They were no longer able to do the will of God. Please read Matthew 13:15.

What was the result of the people's hard hearts?

Jesus desired that His people would return to Him, and He longed to heal them. It is so easy to forget that Jesus longs for us to ask Him for the things we are lacking. In 1 Kings 3:9 Solomon asked God to give him an understanding and discerning heart. God blessed him with more than he asked, and he is remembered as the wisest king who ever lived. In Psalm 86:11 David asked God for an undivided heart. God answered his request, and God called David a man after His own heart. If your heart is lacking, ask God for what you need.

A heart whose passions are aligned with God can't help praising and rejoicing. Below I have listed some praises from the heart. Please read as many as you want, or pick out another favorite Psalm of praise. Take time to thank God for the things He has put in your heart.

Words of praises from the heart: Psalm 9:1, 13:5, 28:7, and Ephesians 5:19-20.

Day 5
A Way with Words

My daughter who is now six years old has always had the ability to just tell things like they are. She speaks the truth without sugar coating it or thinking about consequences. We call her "our little prophet" for this very reason. On the day of our son's adoption, both of my girls were in my bedroom watching me get ready. We were all dressing up fancy because this was a celebration! My daughter who was seven at the time said, "Wow Mom you look hot!" Before I could even respond to her, my four and a half year old said, "Mom you look sweaty." And just like that, I was brought right back down to Earth.

Our speech can be such a complicated issue. Words can have a double meaning. The tone we use with words can also change their meaning. In a world where written communication now dominates, there have been many hurt feelings trying to interpret a message without being able to hear the emotion behind it. The Bible says that from out of the abundance of the heart the mouth speaks (Matthew 12:34). We looked at the heart yesterday. If your heart is filled with sin, your words are bound to cause problems. Please read James 3:2-10.

In verses 3 through 5 James compares the tongue to three illustrations. What is he trying to tell us?

Where does the fire of our tongue originate from (v. 6)? Is that different than any other sin in our life?

In verse 8 it says that no one can tame the tongue. When was the last time you realized how little control you have over your words?

According to verse 8, what is the tongue full of? Give an example of how you have experienced those results in your life.

Why do you think it is possible for both praise and cursing to come out of our mouths?

You may think you have a handle on your thoughts and actions and then something comes out of your mouth that you weren't expecting. We have all been there. James says that no one can tame the tongue so we are all being convicted of this together. We all have memories of words we have said or words spoken to us that had a long lasting impact. I think that is one of the reasons James says the tongue is full of deadly poison. The pain is instant but then it spreads. As my mother would say, "Once a word comes out of your mouth you can never get it back." The damage is done. We tend to think of the sins of our mouth as loud and blatant. Things like uncontrolled anger, yelling, and piercing words are easy to see and get lots of attention. These certainly are sins but there are also sneaky ways our tongue exposes our unrighteousness. Please read Psalm 12:3, Proverbs 11:13, 1 Peter 2:1.

What are some other ways we sin with our words? How can these be just as damaging as the loud outbursts?

The Proverbs are full of wisdom regarding our words. In each of the following Proverbs, there is a benefit and a detriment listed for our words. Please fill in the blanks for each column. Try a couple different translations if the comparison is not clear.

	Benefit	Detriment
Proverbs 10:20	_____	_____
Proverbs 10:32	_____	_____
Proverbs 12:18	_____	_____
Proverbs 14:3	_____	_____
Proverbs 15:1	_____	_____
Proverbs 15:4	_____	_____
Proverbs 18:21	_____	_____

I think the last Proverb sums up everything. Our words bring either life or death. I think the warning for our words is so severe due to the damage that can be caused so quickly. Nothing wields the same power as our tongue. When we sin with our tongue, our sin is always directed at someone else. There are other people that bear the weight of our choices.

Well, there is no way that I could end the lesson here. I have to take you to one final verse. As hard as it is to control our tongues now, it won't always be that way. Our tongues will speak in unison one day.

Please read Philippians 2:9-11. What will our tongues confess?

Yes, there will come a day when our tongues will speak the truth! Amen!

Week 6
Nothing Wasted

Day 1
World of Hurt

   Day 2
   Metamorphosis

      Day 3
      Counting the Costs

         Day 4
         Why Me?

            Day 5
            More Than Able

My family was recycling and composting before it was ever the cool thing to do. Some people recycle for financial reasons and others because it is trendy. God recycles because it is His very nature. He never wastes a moment in our lives. God's abilities are outside the realms of time so He knows how each event in our life will change us into the masterpiece He is creating us to be. This week we will look at all the things God recycles and uses in our lives and discover some limitations to recycled clay. We will also look at how we can be a benefit to others in our lives and learn to trust God more. Don't throw anything away, God can repurpose it all!

Session 6: Viewer Guide
Nothing Wasted

Use It for Good

Absolutely every piece of clay that is not used in a pot gets recycled. God is also in the business of recycling. He will use all our painful experiences, our mistakes, and our trials to work for the good of His children.

1. _____ suffering was for our _____ (Acts 2:23, Hebrews 9:27-28, Hebrews 12:1-3).

2. We are called to _____ for the _____ of others (Genesis 45:1-8, 50:20-21).

3. _____ can help us _____ God's Word (Psalm 119:71).

An Intense Love

1. God's _____ is revealed in the _____ behind His actions.

2. God _____ too much for His people to allow sin to _____ them (Jeremiah 19:1-6, 10-11, 15, Romans 9:25-26).

3. Divine _____ is evidence of _____ love (Hebrews 12:4-11).

Video discussion questions

1. Does knowing Christ had to suffer encourage you in your own suffering?
2. What would it look like to follow Christ's example and endure our suffering with our joy set before us?
3. Joseph was fortunate that he got to see the good come about from his sufferings. This is not always the case. Can God use our pain for good even if we don't get to see it? Have you ever benefited from someone else's pain? Has someone else benefited from your pain?
4. What are some things God has taught you through trials?
5. What can we do when the trial we are facing doesn't make sense to us?
6. Have you ever learned something about God's Word as a result of suffering? What was your insight?
7. Give some examples of how God's divine discipline is evidence of His divine love.

Videos are available for viewing at www.jennykaluza.com/the-potter-and-the-clay-videos.

Day 1
World of Hurt

Recycling is so ingrained in my nature that it is almost embarrassing how many uses I can find for discarded objects. You are very likely to hear me say, "Don't throw that away. I can use that." My house has very little storage, and I think that is God's way of limiting my accumulating abilities. It is a good thing I am such a busy person and don't have a lot of time to spend on the computer because there are now entire websites filled with ideas of how to repurpose old items! A person like me could easily get lost in that world.

When God recycles, it is never because He has to. God recycles because He has a better use for something than how it was originally used in our lives. He is not forcing an event to have an unnatural use like what sometimes happens when I try to reuse a resource in a way it was not intended. God knows how to take our pain and suffering and turn it into beauty. By repurposing the events in our lives, He finds a far greater use than you could ever imagine.

In our video session for this week, I talked about the sources of our suffering. They either come as a result of the Fall and the curses brought upon the Earth, or they are a result of our sinful choices. Sometimes the good things God is doing in our lives still hurt. I want us to review some of the things we have learned in the last couple of weeks.

>   What types of pain come from centering your life to Christ? What pain have you experienced as a result of obedience, pruning your life, working with other Christians and striving for holiness?

>   What types of pain come from God molding and shaping your life? What pain have you experienced as a result of God stretching you beyond your abilities, doing a new thing in your life, or using literal pain to form you into something new?

>   What types of pain come from God removing the excess weight of sin in your life? What pain have you experienced as a result of God preparing you for any good work, separating yourself from the ways of the world, and wearing the yoke of Christ?

Good things can still cause pain. Being set apart and made holy can lead to loneliness and loss, not to mention persecution by those who don't understand our love for God. Please read 1 Peter 3:8-9, 17-18 and 1 Peter 4:12-17.

>   What ways are we to behave in this evil culture (1 Peter 3:8-9)?

Week 6: Nothing Wasted

Why do you think we are still surprised by the persecution of our faith?

When we suffer for the sake of righteousness, we share in the suffering of Christ. What should our response be to this shared suffering? Why (1 Peter 4:13-14)?

If you are going to suffer, it is better to suffer for good than for evil. How does this compare to what Christ did for us (1 Peter 3:18)?

Please read Romans 8:17-18. What is the result if we share in the suffering of Christ?

Seeing the good that is to come helps us endure the pain. We have to have a purpose for why we are suffering, or we might as well suffer for evil. I think that is why a lot of people give up the good fight because they forget what they are fighting for.

I am so thankful for the hindsight that comes with years of trusting in Jesus. Instead of viewing life as an unknowable mystery, I view it as a puzzle that I am only given one piece at a time. The longer I trust Jesus, the more of the puzzle I see come together. High school was not an enjoyable time for me. School was difficult and so were relationships. The high school I attended was in the poorest zip code of our state. There were many single-family homes and kids who had to fend for themselves. I often felt like I was in a world in which I didn't belong. When I went over to friends' houses, I observed family dynamics that I had never seen before. Parents drinking and then driving their kids places, kids cooking dinner, parents leaving at odd hours of the night, and kids allowed to follow after whatever their heart desired. I was scared on more than one occasion. At the time I was not sure God was doing anything more than helping me to endure this time in my life. All I had was one piece of the puzzle. Through the years, I would come to work with many organizations focused on helping the poor. Each job seemed to build on the next and prepare me for what was still to come. While I was working at a homeless shelter, we would often have volunteer groups come in to help for a day. I would watch as several of the Christian groups would struggle with how to fit in and communicate with the homeless women. Here was another piece of my puzzle. God had me endure difficult high school years so I would know how to love and minister to His hurting and broken people.

Please read Romans 5:1-5. What does our suffering produce?

How about you? Has God allowed you to see more than just one piece of your puzzle? God is changing your character one piece at a time. You might be too close to the pieces, but if you step back a moment, I'm confident you will see the bigger picture forming.

77

Day 2
Metamorphosis

I am thankful that God can use my painful experiences for good, but it doesn't surprise me. If I am doing my best to follow after Him and being obedient, of course He would reward me. If anyone was to pick on one of my children and my child responded with love, they would get major praise from me. We might even have to bring out the ice cream!

God certainly uses our suffering for Christ's sake to produce perseverance, character, and hope, but He can also use our sinful choices. Now that completely blows my mind! Rather than letting us simply learn from our mistakes, He can actually turn the mistakes into beauty as well. Before we go any further into this transformation, I want us to look at the areas that we have already studied with the clay these last five weeks that represent our sinful choices.

> What types of pain come from recentering your life to Christ? What pain have you experienced as a result of running away from God and then returning and getting your life back on track?

> What types of pain come from air bubbles (ignored sin)? What pain have you experienced as a result of falling into temptation or ignoring an area of sin in your life? How has other people's sin affected you?

> What types of pain come from carrying the weight of the world? What pain have you experienced as a result of following after the ways of this world rather than the ways of Christ?

One of the differences I see between the areas of pain from yesterday's homework and the areas of pain we are talking about today is the pain from sin lingers. Suffering for righteousness' sake seems to come and go like seasons. There may be times of intense suffering while our character is being developed and then it will be followed by a season of peace. On the other hand, suffering due to sin can last a lifetime. I think that might be another reason our verses from yesterday in 1 Peter Chapters 3 and 4 said it is better to suffer for good than for evil.

Not all sin is used for good. How God uses our sin has everything to do with how we respond when it is revealed in our lives. Please read 2 Chronicles 7:14-15.

> What are four responses to sin listed in this passage that leads to God hearing from Heaven and forgiving sins?

Josiah was a king of Judah. He reigned for thirty-one years. He did what was right in the sight of the Lord. He inherited a rebellious and sinful people as a result of poor leadership that came before him. During his reign, he initiated repairs to the temple. While the repairs were being made, a copy of the Book of the Law was found. Former kings had destroyed all the copies so this was an important find. Please read 2 Kings 22:8-20.

What was Josiah's response upon hearing the words of the Book of the Law (v. 11-13)?

What was God's judgment on Judah (v. 16-17)? Why?

Would King Josiah suffer the same judgment? What actions changed his fate (v. 19-20)?

Josiah's pleas were not enough to change the fate of his country, but they did change his fate. Josiah died in 604 B.C. Four years later Nebuchadnezzar made his first attack on Jerusalem. God responds to a repentant heart. By repenting, we take the first step in allowing our sin to be transformed into something of use.

I love hearing a good testimony. There is nothing more beautiful on this Earth than a repentant sinner. I love seeing how God takes an area of sin in a person's life and turns it into an area of ministry to others. The apostle Paul had a great testimony. Please read 1 Timothy 1:12-17 to hear his story.

How does Paul describe his sin (v. 13 and 15)?

Why would God want to save the worst of sinners? What ministry was Paul able to have after God's grace poured over him (v. 16)?

Paul was the perfect example of what the grace of God can do in a person's life. He called himself the worst of sinners, and his crimes against God and humanity were extreme. Christ still saved him, though. A person who was once proud, arrogant, and violent would be changed into a humble man willing to turn the other cheek. His transformation would bear witness that other sinners could do the same. Sin into beauty! No wonder Paul had to follow these thoughts with the words, "Now to the King, eternal, immortal, invisible, the only God, be honor and glory forever and ever. Amen."

Day 3
Counting the Costs

Now that I have shared a little about my recycling tendencies I am sure you are not at all surprised to learn that I also recycle clay. In this week's video session you saw how I use all clay scraps, trimmings, and dried up broken pieces to make recycled clay. I am careful not to waste anything. Recycled clay has many uses and purposes, and it is still a valuable resource to have. Recycled clay is not new clay, though. Its properties and limitations are different. In general, it is weaker than new clay. I can use it for making smaller items such as mugs and small bowls, but I would never use it to make a large bowl. It doesn't have the same workability and elasticity as new clay.

Our sins are a lot like recycled clay. We do not know what specific consequences our sins will render, but we do know that they will cost us. God never overlooks our sin. It may seem that God has not punished a sin, but He will and the cost may be more than we anticipated. If we are repentant of our sin, God can still use us to accomplish great things for Him. However, our capacity may be different.

In the life of King David we see the perfect example of this. David was king over Israel, and God had given him everything he needed. Still, David wanted more. Rather than going off to war with his men, he stayed behind in his palace. He saw a woman named Bathsheba and wanted her for his own. Even though she was a married woman, David slept with her. She became pregnant. David then had her husband killed to cover up his sin. The prophet Nathan came to confront him. Please read 2 Samuel 12:7-14.

>How did David respond when his sin was revealed? Did God forgive him (V.13)?

>What consequences did David have to suffer (V. 10-14)?

All of the prophecies of Nathan came to pass in David's lifetime and are recorded in the book of 2 Samuel. The first child born to David and Bathsheba did die. One of David's sons, Absalom, drove David out of the city and made himself king. He took David's wives for himself. Three of David's sons died of violent deaths including Absalom. David never anticipated the pain that would come from this season of sin in his life.

However, David was repentant. Even though he still had to suffer the consequences of his sins, God would still work in his life. Please read Psalm 51.

>What elements of remorse do you hear in this Psalm?

> Why do you think we still have to suffer consequences for our sins if we are repentant?

The cost of sin serves as a painful reminder of our shortcomings. The pain motivates us to seek after God's righteousness and deters us from ever wanting to stray from God again. Sometimes after people stray from God, their sin is all they are remembered for. God still loved David, and His greatest gift to humanity would still come through the line of David. David's sin is recorded for all to see, but he is remembered for so much more.

Toward the end of David's life, he gathered all the leaders of Israel to share some of his final thoughts. I would like us to read some excerpts from that speech.

> Please read 1 Chronicles 28:2-3. What were David's plans? In what ways was David limited in his service to God? Why?

> Please read 1 Chronicles 28:6-10. Who was to build the temple and take over as king?

> Look closely at verses 8 through 10. What advice did David give Solomon? How do you think David's experiences shaped the advice he gave?

> Please read 1 Chronicles 28:4 and 28:11-19. In what ways was David still used by God after he sinned? What was he still able to contribute to the temple?

David's life exemplifies that our lives can still be used for great things after seasons of sin if we are repentant. This is an important lesson in our churches. We want to be part of bringing about reconciliation. God is not withholding forgiveness to the repentant and neither should we. Though the original plans we had for our life may be altered, God can still use us for important tasks.

The advice David gave to his son is advice we should all take to heart. "Follow all the commands of the Lord your God and serve Him with wholehearted devotion and a willing mind" (v. 8 and 9). God can repurpose all things in our lives, but just as David had to learn the hard way, obedience is a much easier load to bear than the heavy cost of sin.

Day 4
Why Me?

Human nature is so amusing to me. If a sudden crisis enters our life and we are called on to suffer, our response is often, "Why me?" If, however, one of our loved ones is going through a season of suffering, our response changes to, "Lord, let it be me instead." We are such a fickle group of people. This is exactly why it is best for us not to be in charge of life-altering decisions.

God in His sovereignty uses suffering to accomplish a greater good. He is the only one who knows how to best apply it to bring about His purposes. The suffering may be for your benefit, or it may have nothing to do with you. God in His mercy allows us to ask, "Why me?" but His desire is that we would learn to trust Him. Please read Ephesians 3:7-8 and verse 13.

   Who was Paul suffering for? Why was he willing to endure it?

   Has God ever allowed you to see a greater purpose for your suffering? Who was it for?

Paul's ministry was to preach salvation for the Gentiles. He was not excluding the Jews but rather extending the invitation of God's salvation to all people. This angered the Jews, and Paul was imprisoned for this message. However, if he would have kept silent, the Gentiles would not have heard the Gospel message. This is why Paul said he was suffering for their benefit. The results outweighed the cost.

If we know our suffering is for someone else's benefit, it is easier to endure. It is much harder when we realize that someone else is suffering for our benefit. When I was a junior in high school, the youngest of my five siblings was diagnosed with cancer. He was only five years old at the time. It was an aggressive form of cancer, and the doctors had to fight back hard. He had to undergo grueling tests and aggressive treatments. A good chunk of that next year was spent in the hospital. If I could have changed places with him, I would have done it in a heartbeat. I'm not sure what the rest of my siblings were going through emotionally, but I was a wreck. It was actually easier to go in and watch the tests and treatments than to be at home imagining much worse. I knew I could not bear the weight of this pain on my own. I'm not sure what led me to think that being part of a church could help, but that is what I wanted. My family did not attend church, but I asked my parents if we could go to one. The music teacher at the elementary school where my siblings attended had given my mom the number to her church. My mom had then proceeded to tuck that phone number into a tea kettle for safe keeping. When I asked if we could attend church, she pulled the number out from hiding. We all went together the next Sunday. I don't remember all the sermons that I have heard in my life, but I remember that pastor teaching from Nehemiah. I needed a God who would protect His people.

I would never wish cancer on anyone, but by my brother having cancer our whole family was shaken up. I'm not sure what else would have served as the same kind of wake up call. It drew our family closer to each other and closer to God. For me personally, I know it resulted in my salvation. I may have had a head knowledge of God before this, but now I knew Him in the depths of my soul. I cannot say how that season affected anyone else, but for me, I know my brother's suffering was for my good. Please read 2 Corinthians 1:3-7.

By what names does Paul address God in verse 3?

What role does God assume when we are suffering?

How does God comforting us in turn bless others (v. 4)?

What would change if you viewed your own suffering and discomfort as someone else's benefit and gain?

When Christ comforts us in our suffering, we can then give that same comfort to someone else in a time of need. When I hear about a family who has a child with cancer, my heart instantly goes out to the other siblings in the family. Even though I am now a mom and cannot imagine the pain of watching your child suffer, that is not my experience. I want to make sure that the other children in the family have someone they can talk to and a way to express their feelings. In a situation where they could easily be overlooked, I see them.

What experiences have you had in your life that allows you to comfort others?

Learning to view our suffering for the benefit of others does not change our situation. We will still have to endure our trial. It does, however, change our outlook. Hope and purpose give meaning to what we are going through and strengthens us to persevere. If you are facing a trial right now, look around and see who might be benefiting from you. On the other hand, if you are benefiting by someone else's trial, let them know. This glimmer of hope could be just what they need to confirm they are doing God's will. Our sufferings are not meant to be carried alone. "And our hope for you is firm, because we know that just as you share in our sufferings, so also you share in our comfort" (2 Corinthians 1:7).

Day 5
More Than Able

Because I have such a great love for God's Word, it always bothers me when it is taken out of context or used incorrectly. Even worse is when something is credited as being from the Bible, and it doesn't even exist in the text! Often when a fellow Christian is suffering, someone will encourage them with the words, "God never gives us more than we can handle." It takes so much restraint on my part not to jump right out of my seat. Nowhere in God's Word does it say that. Please read 1 Corinthians 10:13.

Of what does God say He won't give us more than we can handle?

Whew! I feel much better getting that off my chest. Just like suffering, temptation will come to everyone. Unlike suffering, we are not called to stay put in our temptation but to flee from them. God never gives us more temptation than we can handle, and He always provides a way out.

This same promise is not made of suffering. Telling someone who is crumbling under the weight of their suffering that God never gives them more than they can handle, implies that they are strong enough on their own. God absolutely gives us more than we can handle! That is the whole point. We can't handle it on our own. Yesterday we read 2 Corinthians 1:3-7. I want to finish that passage by having us read 2 Corinthians 1:8-11.

How does Paul describe the depth of their suffering in verse 8?

Why did God allow them to suffer so severely (v. 9)?

What did Paul say was an encouragement in their time of suffering (v.11)?

This passage is so rich. God gave Paul more than he could handle. Paul's suffering was so severe he thought he was going to physically die. The word death is used several times in this passage. The original Greek word for "death" is *thanatos*. It means "the death of the body, the separation of the soul and the body by which the life on earth is ended."[1] Paul was not simply using this phrase to help elaborate a point. When God intervened and saved him, he saw it as being saved from literal death. Paul thanked the church in Corinth for their prayers. By partnering with Paul in prayer they were also able to rejoice with Paul over God's deliverance. Paul did not question why he was given more than he could handle but knew it was in order that he would place his trust in God who would raise him from the dead should he die.

Week 6: Nothing Wasted

I tend to have a stubborn streak. I admit it. If something can be done with my own strength, that is what I will rely on. Five years ago my husband and I bought a house, and it has been nothing but trouble. We have had heating, plumbing, electrical, and mold problems. At one point the only room on our house that wasn't under construction was our bathroom. After two straight years of working on it, we were finally ready to hang some drywall. We went in to apply for our final permit only to be told we needed an entirely new drain field for our septic system before we could put up the drywall. That was the proverbial straw that broke the camel's back. I lost it. I had been raising my small children in a house filled with framing studs for two years and working as hard as I physically could. I could not bear this anymore. When I got home, I marched straight to the basement and abandoned myself to prayer. I'm quite sure the neighbors could have heard me. I prayed in Jesus' name that Satan would have no grips on our home and that this house would be used for God's glory. While I was praying the phone rang; it was the inspector. He had a cancelation and could come to our home right away. When he arrived, he remembered me from a previous inspection. I had been kind to him which apparently leaves an impression in his line of work. He gave us the approval we needed, and the drywall was hung that week. I would like to tell you that I learned my lesson, but God has had to take me to my limit several times before I've surrendered. My prayer is that relying on Jesus would be my first instinct and not my fall back plan. When God gives us more than we can handle, we learn that He is worthy of our trust. Please read 1 Peter 2:4-6.

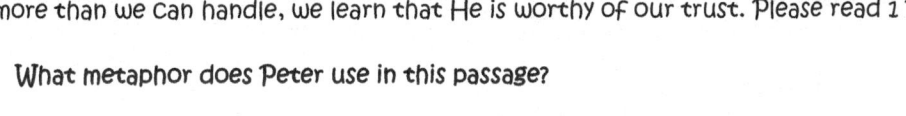

What metaphor does Peter use in this passage?

What is being built? And what is being offered?

What is the result of believing and trusting in Jesus?

As we mature in Christ we are built into a spiritual house. Our sacrifices are no longer the animal sacrifices associated with the Law, but instead, we offer spiritual sacrifices. When we trust Jesus, it is a spiritual sacrifice, and we will not be disappointed. If we are doing things in our strength, the world sees our abilities. If we are doing things in the strength of God, the world sees God's abilities. This is why we are given more than we can handle. The world needs to see what only God can do.

The next time you see a believer suffering from a heavy burden, pray for them. Encourage them to be in God's Word. You also can be in God's Word on their behalf. God's Word is new each time we read it because each time we have a new need. The One who is more than able will not disappoint, and you can join in rejoicing when His purpose is fulfilled. Rest assured His purposes are being fulfilled. In what God is building, nothing is wasted.

Week 7
Mud is Messy

Day 1
They Will Know We are Christians

Day 2
Love Your Neighbor

Day 3
Loving Our King

Day 4
One Nation Under God

Day 5
Seventy Times Seven

I love watching kids do art. They are not good at hiding their emotions so you know immediately how they feel about the project. I especially like a messy project. Some kids will instantly dive in and end up wearing more of the project than whatever makes it on to the paper. Other kids won't touch the mess. They may poke it with a stick, but their response is usually, "Ew, gross!" As we mature our responses may outwardly be more hidden, but inwardly they are just the same. This week we get to look at the incredible mess of human relationships. God has called us to love each other, but it is difficult and messy. God's Word has much to teach us about how to show His love to others and the benefits of getting messy. So put on your art aprons, we are diving in!

Session 7: Viewer Guide
Mud is Messy

Mud is Messy

1. _____ is messy.

Vine's Expository Dictionary defines mercy as the "outward manifestation of pity".[1] Mercy is God's attitude and response towards those in distress.

2. God gave us _____ when we deserved _____. (Romans 5:6-8)

3. Jesus came to be a _____ for the _____. (Matthew 9:10-13)

Willing to Get Messy

1. Jesus _____ us to _____ _____ to others.

2. Showing mercy will get us _____. (Luke 10:30-37)

3. Showing mercy will require us to _____ _____. (vs. 34-35)

You can prepare for mercy in three ways.

    A. You are prepared by being _____ _____ (vs. 34).

    B. You are prepared with _____ _____ (vs. 34-35).

    C. You are prepared with good _____ _____ (vs. 35).

4. Showing mercy is a _____ for all not just those with the _____ _____ (Luke 10:25, 10:37).

5. Showing mercy is different from _____.

6. The greatest way we show mercy is by _____ _____ _____.
(Matthew 28:19-20)

Judgment Versus Mercy

1. God asks us to show mercy to others in _____ to the mercy He _____ us. (Matthew 18:21-35)

2. _____ triumphs over _____. (Matthew 5:7, James 2:12-13)

Video discussion questions
1. Have you ever had someone believe in your potential even if you hadn't proved it yet? How did it make you feel?
2. God asks us to show mercy to others in comparison to the mercy He gave us. What does that look like?
3. I gave examples of three ways we can be prepared to show mercy. Can you think of other ways?
4. Why would justice be easier to give than mercy? Why are we so driven for justice?
5. James 2:13 states that "mercy triumphs over justice." Why is that? Why should we err on the side of mercy?
6. If we all agree that God's Word commands us to be merciful to others, those needing mercy are still messy. What are practical ways we can learn to get messy? How do we become comfortable with loving the "sick"?

Videos are available for viewing at www.jennykaluza.com/the-potter-and-the-clay-videos.

Day 1
They Will Know We are Christians

Growing up I listened to a lot of Amy Grant's music. She had one album that had several songs about loving others. I typed out the lyrics to her song "Father's Eyes" and hung it on my bulletin board. I prayed that God would allow me to see others the way He saw them. I do believe He answered that prayer by giving me a heart of mercy. There was another song on that album called "Giggle." The song talked about loving someone who didn't smell good and the giggles of your peers. As much as I wanted to love people the way God loved them, I was also swayed heavily by peer pressure. I desperately wanted to be liked in high school, and that didn't always lead to the wisest of decisions. I remember one day in my freshman social studies class like it was yesterday. The teacher was dividing us into groups to work on a project. I had several friends in the class that I wanted to impress, but I was not put in their group. Instead, I was paired with a boy that no one knew. He smelled bad and did not seem to have many clothes. Looking back, I'm sure the teacher paired me with him thinking that I would be kind to him. Unfortunately, that was not the choice I made. Instead, I positioned my body as far as I could from him and spent the day looking over my shoulder at my group of friends. Thinking back on my behavior I still shudder. The friends I was trying to impress were not kind people, and I would never fully be included in their group. I often wonder about that boy, though. What kind of impact could I have had if I would have chosen kindness? Did anyone ever show him love? Loving others is hard, but if we can't love human beings how can we expect to love God? Please read 1 John 4:7-21.

Where does love originate? When you show love for others what does that say about your faith in God (v. 7)?

Is it possible to love God but not love others? Why or why not?

God set an example to show us what love is. Based on His example, what do you think our love should look like?

How does love between Christians make the love of God visible (v. 12-16)?

Why do you think it should be easier to love a fellow Christian than an invisible God?

Discussing love can be a confusing topic until we define it. The love described in this passage is not a feeling or emotion. Unlike English, in Greek, there are different words for the different types of love. The Greek word used for "love" in this passage is *agapao*. Agapao is used to express the love God has for Jesus and human beings.[2] This is the type of love God desires to be evident among believers. Agapao is the verb-form of the noun agape. This type of love is evident in the actions it prompts and by obedience to God. God displayed His agapao love for us when He sent Jesus to die on the cross. This is the type of love that is the fruit of the Spirit (Galatians 5:22). Agapao is not just a love for those you are naturally drawn to but a love for all humanity.

Having this definition in mind, please read through 1 John 4:7-21 one more time. We can only have this type of love towards humankind by having God's Holy Spirit indwell us. This type of love is in contrast to the love that is so freely displayed in movies and music. This love goes against natural instincts. Therefore when it is present, the qualities of God are made visible. If God's Spirit is in you, so will His love also be in you. The Spirit within a person is revealed in their actions. Please read Matthew 22:36-39.

In your own words please state the greatest commandment.

Guess what type of love Jesus is commanding of us? You got it, agapao. This is the command that John restated in 1 John 4:21. Loving God and loving each other go hand in hand. Please read John 13:34-35.

Who is Jesus talking to in the passage? Look back over the chapter for clues.

Agapao love is certainly important to all humanity, but why would it be especially necessary among believers?

Trials bring out the best and the worst in people. I can only imagine the emotions that would be evident during the severe persecution that would quickly befall all Christians after Jesus' death. They would need a supernatural love to hold them together. The love they were to have for each other would show the world what God's love looks like.

Just because a person is a Christian does not make their personality more like yours or make them easier to be around. We will all still annoy each other. God wants His love to flow out of us in a particular order. First, we are to love God, then other believers, then all of humanity. Christians are to be in community with one another. That community should completely stand out from the world around it. Those who have only experienced the love of this world should want what they see in us. Please end today by thanking God for the love a fellow believer has shown you.

Describe a time when another Christian showed you agapao love? What effect did it have on you?

Day 2
Love Your Neighbor

When I first met my husband, he was a mechanic. He later got a degree in computer networking. You can only imagine how popular he is with our friends and neighbors. You will often see him hopping the fence to fix a lawn mower, snow blower, car engine, or any other mechanical device that a neighbor needs help with. If his hands aren't busy, he is on the phone helping walk through a computer, tablet, or camera problem to any number of our friends. When the phone rings, very rarely does someone need me. He is the very picture of what it means to be a servant. Please read Mark 10:43-45.

Why is it important to have a servant's heart?

Jesus never asks us to do something that He hasn't already done first. The needs of this world can be overwhelming. One person cannot possibly do it all. When the needs are so great, it can almost immobilize you in the uncertainty of where to begin. In the sea of needs, a good place to start looking is at your neighbor. Please read Galatians 5:13-14.

Why do you think it is important to have our service tied to our love?

What is the summation of the law?

Please read Romans 13:8-10. How does loving your neighbor cover all of the laws?

I so hope you were able to do yesterday's lesson. The same love we learned about yesterday is the same word used today. We are called to love our neighbors with an agapao love. In our selfish nature, most of us would not delight in pouring ourselves out in service to our neighbors. And as we learned in our video session, anyone with a need is our neighbor. Only through the love of the Holy Spirit pouring through us can we love our neighbors selflessly.

I find it interesting that we are commanded to love our neighbors as ourselves, not love them as we would friends or family. It is quite telling that the thing we treat the best is ourselves. When we love our neighbor to that extent, we cause no harm to our neighbor, therefore, love is the only commandment we need. It is important to remember that the only love that causes no harm is the love that comes from God.

Throughout the Bible, God makes it clear that not only does He love a servant's heart, but He loves the less fortunate. He loves all of His creation. When some of His children are not being taken care of, He takes it personally. Please read Psalm 35:10, 113:7-8, and 140:12.

What are God's feelings toward the poor?

To ensure that the poor, widows, and orphans were taken care of, several laws in the Old Testament outlined their treatment. Please read Leviticus 19:9-10 and 25:35-41.

What were some of the practices that ensured the poor were taken care of?

A compassion for the poor was also evident in the New Testament. The source of the motivation for taking care of the poor shifted. Rather than being motivated by keeping the law, New Testament believers were to be motivated by a love for others.

Please read Luke 12:32-34. How do these verses represent a heart issue rather than a law issue?

Please read James 1:27 and 2:1-8. What problems was James addressing?

What solution did James offer for these problems (v. 8)?

God desires that all of His children would experience His love. Christians are the avenue in which Christ meets those needs. The law was once necessary to ensure the kind treatment of those less fortunate. Christ came to fulfill the law (Matthew 5:17). Through His life, He showed us what it means to serve others. Christ desires that we would be motivated out of our love for Him to serve those He loves.

We live in a society where one of the first phrases children learn to utter is, "Mine." We like to work hard and then feel entitled to what we have earned. Our government has programs to ensure that all the poor are fed and provided for. Why should we feel the need to get involved? The treasure we are storing away on this Earth will not last. It serves no other purpose than to meet a very temporal pleasure. God wants us to join in service with Him so we can also experience the blessing with Him. When we meet the needs of each other, it binds us together. Both the giver and receiver are built up. We all have needs. One person's may be financial while another's are emotional. Being part of the body of Christ means that when everyone is contributing, all of Christ's flock is flourishing. Go out and meet your neighbors!

Day 3
Loving Our King

Zach and I did not have a typical dating relationship. God made it quite clear before we ever started dating that we would indeed be each other's spouses. I made a few things quite clear up front as well. I had Zach volunteer where I was working so he could see the kind of kids and families my heart breaks for. I love kids who are a little rough around the edges. I'm okay if I have to earn their trust before they show affection. My heart breaks for women who have made bad life decisions and have had their children removed from their care as a result. I want to be part of the reconciliation process. I want to partner with Christ to mend the broken-hearted. Before we ever had children of our own, Zach knew I wanted our family to be open to foster kids.

We were very purposeful in having our biological children first so they could set an example for the children who would be entering our home. I was well trained, and we thought we knew what we were getting into. We have been foster parents for three years now, and nothing could have prepared us for the mess of the state foster care system. I learned quickly the difference between dealing with messy people at work and dealing with messes in your home. It is a very difficult task to love a baby as if it was your own, the whole time knowing they could leave any day. It is difficult to love the parents who caused harm to the child, help train them to be equipped as parents, and at the same time never wanting to give the baby back. After caring for a little baby boy for 18 months, we were able to adopt him. Adoption does not mean the mess is over. We have an open adoption so we will be in contact with his biological parents for life. Our son will know he is adopted. We know there will be many hard conversations, not to mention the fear of one day losing him. What a mess!

You may be asking why we would ever choose this? It is only because I know the answer to that question so clearly that I am able to continue with this passion.

Please read 2 Corinthians 5:13-15. What do you think it means to have Christ's love compel you?

What have you done out of your love for God that others thought was crazy?

I know I am out of my mind. What our family is doing makes no sense unless it is out of our love for Jesus. It is way too hard, emotional, and inconvenient to live this way if not for the compelling love within us. If we are going to follow Christ, we first have to die to ourselves (Mark 8:35). This type of love will not make sense to everyone. Please read 1 Corinthians 1:18-25.

Why would the message of the cross be foolishness to those who don't believe?

How do God's wisdom and strength compare to ours?

God gives all abilities and strength. He is not against intelligent thought and reason. In fact, God tells us to ask for wisdom if we lack it. God wants us to use our brain. The problem comes when a person thinks they are wiser or greater than God. God's ways are not our ways. His thoughts are higher and greater than ours (Isaiah 55:9). Faith is required for belief, and to those who trust only in their mind, that is foolishness.

Well, simply being a little out of our minds would not be enough to sustain us for lifelong service. Often the results of all our efforts are never seen and can be discouraging. What happens if a parent is not changed for the better? What happens if the child's life is not improved? What if we are doing all this work and nothing ever changes? Does it still matter? Please read Matthew 25:31-40.

Why is our love for the needy never wasted?

What area of service in your life could this verse encourage you in?

We will not get to see the results of all our labor, but it is not wasted. Every act of love to someone in need is received by Christ as if we did that very thing to Him. It is clear the benefits that come from serving others, but I also have a word of caution. Those with a gift of service can easily start serving out of their own strength. When this happens, exhaustion is inevitable and the love grows weak. Our service to the needy can only come from Christ's love compelling us. It has to be from a place of overflow. It is His strength and abilities we have to rely on. Christ desires that our love for others would be lifelong. Our strength will not last a lifetime, and burn out will most certainly happen if we are not tapping into an eternal source.

Though we are all called to serve, I am certainly not implying that all should be foster parents. It is important that your area of service be an area of passion and one that fits your family's needs. Before we take a child into our home, every member of our family has a vote. If the needs within our family are too great, we do not add to the burden. This type of service also uniquely fits the gifting of each member of our family including our children. This is important to me because I want them to learn to use their spiritual gifts as well. One of our daughters has the gifts of mercy and service. She willingly holds babies and enjoys meeting their needs. Our other daughter has the gift of evangelism. I love hearing her witness to the guests who stay in our home. Zach's gift of service is evident in the way he supports each member of our family. I get to use my gifts to teach the parents about Christ and pray with them in their time of need. Our lifestyle does not make sense unless you realize we aren't doing it for our benefit. We are just loving our King. When you love others you are loving Christ.

Day 4
One Nation Under God

I tend to buy a lot of my clothes at thrift stores. I love finding a good deal, and the price helps our family stay on budget. After selling a car that I dearly loved in order to downsize our vehicles, my husband set aside some money for me to buy a new pair of Dansko shoes. Normally, I would never spend that much on shoes so this was a real treat. I had only worn them a couple of times when my oldest daughter decided to pour olive oil all inside of them and on my pillow. She was obviously upset with me, and this was her method of letting me know. After I regained my composure, I called Zach and said, "You will never believe what your daughter did!" I was letting him know that this behavior had to come from his side of the gene pool. This would not be the last time I would utter this phrase concerning the behavior of our children.

Moses had a household of his own to take care of, but he also was the leader of the nation of Israel. Being put in charge of this nation would make any parenting job look easy. Moses had to deal with their grumblings about being hungry and thirsty. They grumbled again when they grew tired of God's miracle manna. When Moses left them for forty days to receive the Ten Commandments from God, they did not wait patiently. Please read Exodus 32:1-10.

How did Israel respond to the absence of Moses?

What did God call the nation of Israel in verse 7?

What was God's plan for the nation? What did God offer Moses (v. 10)?

Oh, how God's response in verse 7 makes me laugh. See, my response was biblical! God refused to claim His people as His own or claim responsibility for bringing them out of Egypt due to their outrageous behavior. Instead, God passes Israel off as Moses' people and responsibility. Even though they did not have the Ten Commandments written in stone yet, Moses had already shared the law with them verbally. They knew what they were doing was wrong. God was so angered by their behavior He planned to destroy them. He then proposed to Moses that He would make a great nation out of Moses. This had to be an incredibly tempting thought to Moses considering all he had put up with. Please read Moses' response in Exodus 32:11-13.

How did Moses refer to the people of Israel in these verses?

What did he ask of God on Israel's behalf?

Please read Exodus 32:14. How did God respond to Moses' request?

Instead of abandoning his people, Moses intervenes on their behalf. He refers to Israel as God's people and reminds God of His covenantal promise to Abraham, Isaac, and Jacob. God already knew these things, but He allowed Moses to be part of the plan. Disaster was avoided for Israel because Moses pleaded on their behalf, and God dearly loved Moses.

All throughout the Old Testament, leaders, prophets, and kings sought favor with the Lord, intervening on behalf of Israel. Please read Daniel 9:1-23.

How does Daniel refer to the sins of his people? Pay close attention to verses 5, 8, 11, and 15.

Everything we know about Daniel points to him being a righteous man. He knew the Scriptures. It was because of his knowledge of God's Word that he knew the time of Israel's captivity would soon end. It was these events that drove him to his knees. Not only did he pray for his people, but he included himself in their sin. He didn't say, "They have rebelled." He instead said, "We have sinned, we have been wicked, we have rebelled, and we have not listened." He was so passionate about the welfare of his people that he included himself in their sin.

People are so messy. They make bad choices, and they fail God miserably. We all are in the same boat. Without the mercy and grace of our God, we would be helpless to help ourselves. When was the last time you prayed for your nation? What elements of Moses and Daniel's prayers can you incorporate into your pleas for your people? God listens to the pleas of the righteous. As soon as Daniel began praying, God responded.

Take time to write down a prayer for your nation, leaders, and church.

Intercession is not just an Old Testament idea. Please read Romans 8:34.

Who is interceding for you?

I cannot imagine a more comforting thought than the reality that Jesus intercedes for me. Even while Jesus was hanging on the cross, He continued to intercede. "Father, forgive them, for they do not know what they are doing" (Luke 23:34).

Day 5
Seventy Times Seven

Teaching the concept of forgiveness to an adult is a difficult task. Teaching this concept to a child seems like an insurmountable task. Forgiveness is a heart issue. I can teach my children to say the words, "I'm sorry I hurt you, please forgive me." They can also learn the appropriate response of, "I forgive you." Though the words may be correct, the looks on their faces tell a different story.

I think one of the hardest components of relationships is learning to forgive. Forgiveness does not mean that everything goes back to the way it was before the offense. It also doesn't mean you won't be wronged again. Forgiveness is necessary for reconciliation with others, but it is also necessary for your relationship with Christ. We will study three benefits and reasons forgiveness is so vital in the life of every believer.

1. The first reason forgiveness is important is because Christ forgives us, and we are to be a reflection of Christ. Christ wants us to show forgiveness to others in the same measure that it was given to us. While Jesus was sharing His last meal with His disciples, He gave them a visual illustration to represent the work that He would do for them on the cross.

   Please read Matthew 26:26-28. What work was Jesus' death going to accomplish?

   Please read Matthew 18:21-22. What was Jesus saying by using such a large number to represent forgiveness?

When Jesus died on the cross, it was a payment for all sins. The payment would not need to be repeated. The grace that comes from the work on the cross is sufficient to cover all past, present, and future sins. Jesus' ability to forgive you never ends. We are being made into the image of Christ. Jesus desires that we would show forgiveness to others in the same extent to which it is given to us. When Peter asked Jesus to give him a number of how many times he should forgive, Jesus responded with, "Seventy times seven" (NASB). Jesus did not intend for Peter to count up to 490 offenses but rather gave him a number that was too large to possibly keep track of. Our forgiveness to others is to be limitless because Christ sets no limits on us.

2. The second reason forgiving others is important is that it is tied to our fellowship with God. Jesus taught His disciples how they should pray. In the prayer, we learn elements of forgiveness. Please read Matthew 6:9-15.

   Why does Jesus say it is important to forgive others before coming to God in prayer?

It is important to point out that the forgiveness of our sins which leads to salvation is a result of us repenting from our sins, putting our faith in Jesus, believing God's Word, and confessing our beliefs. We went over this in great detail in week 3. This passage is not speaking about the salvation of the believer but rather the fellowship that we have with God after we are saved. If you are holding back forgiveness from someone, you need to offer them forgiveness before coming and seeking forgiveness from God. Your fellowship with God will suffer as a result of the unforgiveness you are harboring.

3. Lastly, forgiveness is important so we can live in the freedom of Christ. Harboring unforgiveness in your heart leads to other areas of sin. Bitterness can grow like a cancer poisoning all aspects of your life. Please read Ephesians 4:29-32.

What actions grieve (sadden) the Holy Spirit?

What is the solution given in verse 32?

Please read Luke 6:37-42. How does unforgiveness cause us to have a plank in our eye?

When we refuse to forgive, bitterness, anger, and resentment grow. Often we are blinded by our own sin because we are so focused on the wrong that was done to us. Forgiving others frees us to experience all of the blessings that come from our relationship with Christ.

I usually get along well with all types of people. This makes it very easy to love them. Loving your enemies is another story. It is very difficult to love someone when they hate you. It is very difficult to forgive when someone is not seeking your forgiveness. Our family had a very difficult relationship with some neighbors of ours. One summer it got so bad we could not go outside without our neighbors climbing the fence and yelling obscenities at us. I would get physically sick from the anxiety this relationship caused. My solution was to move, my husband's solution was to seek reconciliation. Following his leadership, we wrote our neighbors a letter telling them that we desired to reconcile with them and asked for forgiveness for any wrong we had done. I was initially very opposed to writing this letter. They should be the ones apologizing, not us. Thankfully I chose submission over stubbornness. Our neighbors never responded to the letter, but their behavior changed dramatically. Within a month they were inviting us over to their house for a Labor Day party. I didn't realize how much anger and bitterness I was holding on to until peace returned. My unforgiveness was causing me to sin. I was so focused on the wrong that was done to me that I was blinded to all the ways I was allowing sin to control me. Loving messy people means we are going to have to learn the art of forgiveness.

Are you harboring any unforgiveness in your heart? Write out a plan to deal with it.

Week 8
Signed and Sealed

Day 1
Wonderfully Made

Day 2
Taste and See

Day 3
Bride of Christ

Day 4
Our Father Which Art in Heaven

Day 5
A Little More Undignified

I never was able to take an art history class, but I would love to. I love that there are characteristics so unique to each artist that after studying their work you can identify their pieces without seeing the signature. Their method becomes their signature. If a stranger can identify an artist's work, just think how much easier it is for the artist. This week we will discover the depth that we are known by our Potter. We will also learn new ways to get to know Him in return. Creativity isn't something that is only helpful in art. It will also help us to know our God in new and exciting ways.

Session 8: Viewer Guide
Signed and Sealed

Engraved Hands

1. It is _____ for God to _____ His people (Isaiah 49:14-16).

2. Our knowledge of God is tied loosely with _____ on our hands in comparison to God's knowledge of us that is _____ into His hands (Deuteronomy 6:4-8).

3. By His _____ we are _____ (1 Peter 2:23-24).

Signed, Sealed and Delivered

1. God has set His _____ on His children, claiming _____ of His possession (2 Corinthians 1:21-22).

2. We are sealed with the _____ _____ the moment we _____ the Gospel message (Ephesians 1:13-14).

3. The Holy Spirit is a _____ guaranteeing our _____ of eternal life with Christ (2 Corinthians 1:22, Ephesians 1:14).

Known By Name

1. God _____ us by _____ (Exodus 33:17).

2. God calls us by the _____ He is _____ in us (Isaiah 43:1).

3. We can only _____ to God calling us by name if we know His _____ (John 10:1-11).

Video discussion questions
1. What is the meaning of your name?
2. What are some strategies you use to help you remember things? Is it still possible for you to forget? What does it mean when God says, "I will not forget you"? What impact does this promise have on you?
3. Why do you think Jesus kept His scars after the resurrection?
4. What are some ways the Holy Spirit prevents us from being tampered with?
5. What are some ways you are assured that you belong to God? How do you know if you have the Holy Spirit?
6. The gifts of the Spirit are numerous (fruit of the Spirit, spiritual gifts). What is your reaction to these things only being a deposit of what is to come?
7. Have you ever studied an art or a hobby long enough to recognize the artist without seeing the signature? Think of some current people like Mary Engelbreit or street artist Banksy. What makes their work identifiable? What makes Christians identifiable?
8. What are some things that only God could know about you because He made you?

Videos are available for viewing at www.jennykaluza.com/the-potter-and-the-clay-videos.

Day 1
Wonderfully Made

The desire to be known is one the strongest human yearnings. It is what drives us to seek out friendships and relationships. We can get instantly frustrated when either a friend who has known us for a great length of time or our spouse acts in a manner that exposes their limited knowledge of us. It is impossible for any human to ever completely know us. It is this desire that also drives us to search for God. We crave to be known completely, and we know that no other human can fill that need so we set out to find what can.

God is the only one who can know us completely. The depth of His understanding of us is limitless. He knows things about us that even we ourselves do not know. He knows our name and our character, but He also knows every detail of our life. Psalm 139 contains a beautiful description of God's knowledge of us. This is the only passage we will be reading today. I would like you to read the psalm in its entirety and then read it in another translation. We will then focus on the individual parts. Please take a moment to read it now.

Six times in this psalm David uses some form of the word "know." The original Hebrew word for "know" is *yada*. It means "to know, to perceive and see, discriminate, distinguish, discern, to know by experience, to be acquainted with, to be wise, and to reveal."[1] This type of knowledge is much more than an intellectual knowledge, it is an intimate knowledge. In the Bible when it refers to a husband and a wife knowing each other and then bearing children, *yada* is the word that is used. Marital relationships are the most intimate relationships on earth, and yet even that knowledge does not compare to God's knowledge of us.

   Search verses 2 through 4 and list everything that God knows about us.

   Have you ever been overwhelmed or scared by the amount of knowledge God has?

   How might verses 5 through 12 expose nervousness on David's part of God's intimate knowledge of him?

Depending on what tone you read this passage with, you can interpret two different meanings. An awareness of God's all-knowing ability will either draw us close to Him or create an urgency to escape and hide. In verse 6, David refers to God's knowledge as too wonderful for him. Wonderful in this context means it is beyond human understanding.

In verses 2 through 9 David uses five extremes to represent the complete knowledge and presence of God. Below I have listed all of those phrases and which verses they can be found in. Next to each phrase please fill in what you think it represents.

Week 8: Signed and Sealed

Verse 2: Sit and rise _____

Verse 3: Going out and lying down _____

Verse 5: Behind and before _____

Verse 8: Heavens and depths _____

Verse 9: Dawn and dusk _____

God sees all actions and every part of our day. There is no direction where He cannot be found. Rather than wanting to escape that presence, David was comforted that God's knowledge of him began long before he was aware of it.

David shifted his attention in verses 13 through 18 to God's creation of him. Which aspects of creation was David in awe over?

I love a good dramatic twist, but all of a sudden in verses 19 through 22, David switched from how vast and wonderful the knowledge of God is, to wanting God to avenge his enemies who were also enemies of God.

Why would recognizing the Lord's presence shift your focus to your enemies?

If God knows all things, He also knows our present conditions. David had already acknowledged that God knew his every thought and every word before he spoke. Rather than hide his concerns, he openly shares his feelings and fears with God. David ends this psalm with a slightly different twist than how he started it. Please compare verse 1 with 23 and 24.

How are these verses similar and how are they different?

What comforts do you find in God knowing you completely?

At the start of the psalm, David acknowledges that God has searched him. After pondering the ways and nature of God, David asks to be searched. It is no longer just a fact, but David is now inviting God in, craving intimacy with his God.

Being known can be our greatest desire or our greatest fear. Jesus' love covers us so there is no condemnation for those who are in Christ (Romans 8:1). Take comfort in the God who knows all about you and loves you completely.

Day 2
Taste and See

We have looked in depth at all the ways God knows us. Jeremiah 1:5 states, "Before I formed you in the womb I knew you, before you were born I set you apart." Our goal is to know Him in return. For the remainder of the week, we will discover ways we can know God. It is impossible for us to know Him the same way He knows us while we are here on Earth, but we can strive toward that goal. Please read 2 Corinthians 3:12-18.

Describe the change that happens when we believe in Christ as described in verse 18?

When Moses was in the presence of the Lord, his face radiated with God's glory. The glory was not lasting though; it faded over time. Those whose faith is in Christ will have an increasing glory and radiance. It does not fade or dim but only increases over time as we are sanctified and transformed into the image of Christ. The more we are made like Him the more glimpses we get to see of Him. Please read 1 Corinthians 13:8-12.

What happens as we mature? How did Paul use verses 8 through 11 to describe this process?

Verse 12 represents a change happening. What things change?

Paul used the image of a mirror in our passage from 1 Corinthians 13 to help explain a point. Depending on which translation you read from, the 2 Corinthians 3 passage uses the image of a mirror as well. I was always a bit confused as to why the image in the mirror was referred to as a dim reflection. When I look at the image in my mirror, it might not be perfect, but it is a pretty good representation. This is where context is so important. In Biblical times they did not use glass mirrors. The city of Corinth, to whom Paul was writing, was famous for their large bronze mirrors.[2] There would certainly be a likeness but many things would be distorted. Think of it as looking into a metal frying pan. You might be able to recognize the face, but the reality is so much better. This is what our knowledge of God will be like. Now we can only know in part, but eventually we will have perfect knowledge.

Please read 1 John 3:1-2. What are Christians referred to as in these verses?

How do these verses explain why we are called children?

We do not know what our final transformation will be like, but we do know when. When does our final transformation happen (v. 2)?

Please read John 17:1-3. What is the definition of eternal life?

Eternal life is being able to fully know God. No longer is the image distorted. We will see Jesus face to face!

What questions are you most excited to ask Jesus when you get to Heaven?

There is a reason we long for Heaven. There are limitations to life on this Earth. However, if we spend our whole lives waiting for Heaven we will miss out on special moments of intimacy we can have right now.

In last week's homework I had us look at the final meal Christ shared with His disciples. At the meal, Jesus broke the bread and told His disciples, "Take and eat; this is my body." Then He took the wine and said drink, "This is my blood of the covenant, which is poured out for many for the forgiveness of sins" (Matthew 26:26-28). I want to take you to an Old Testament passage that has a similar message.

Please read Psalm 34:8. How do we know that the Lord is good?

This is not some weird form of cannibalism. This is an experiential relationship. Our relationship with Christ can involve all of our senses. If you are having trouble sensing the presence of God, it is time for you to taste and see! It is time to mix up the old routines. God is not silent. He longs for us to seek after Him, and He will make Himself known.

The idea of a personal relationship with Christ is not a new concept, and yet we keep trying to fit Him in the same old box. I am so excited to journey with you through the next three days of our study. We are going to look at how studying God's Word, our prayer life, and our worship can evolve to new depths when we shake up our routine.

During my student teaching for my education degree, we learned all the different ways the human brain learns new information. There are all different styles of learning. The more styles of learning that are incorporated into a lesson, the more information is retained. And guess what happens the more our senses are incorporated into our learning? You guessed it. There is a reason so many of our memories include food! When you taste and see, you will find out that the Lord is good!

Day 3
The Bride of Christ

Dating relationships are a tricky thing. I was absolutely no good at dating. There is a fascinating thing that happens during the senior year at a Christian college, everyone becomes engaged. Thankfully I found three Christian ladies who were just as single as I was. Rather than heading to the altar, we set off on adventures. It was fun while it lasted, but one by one they too got engaged and moved away. At the time, I was one of just a few single women at my work so all the other women were eager to set me up with their son or relative. I was so desperate to join the ranks of all my friends that I agreed to go on my one and only blind date.

Unfortunately, I don't remember the name of the man I had the blind date with. He will forever be known to me as "the fish man." He was nice and the conversation was pleasant, but I was not feeling a major connection with him. During the course of our conversation, he brought up the fact that he had a phobia. He was deathly afraid of fish. I have never been known to have a great poker face, and upon him revealing his fears I let out a laugh! I had to explain to him that it was not his fear that was funny but rather the blatant message God was sending me. You see, I love fish. I am a scuba diver. Every room in my house has decorations of either water or fish. As a child, I would pretend I was a mermaid. God could not have sent me a more direct message. This was not the man for me, and this was not my time to be dating. God wanted my attention, and He wanted to be my date.

I wasn't quite sure what to do next. I knew Jesus was calling me to a more personal relationship with Him, and I was not meant to date anyone yet. How could I get to know Him better? I simply thought about the people I knew best and how I got to know them. I then tried to figure out how I could apply that to my relationship with Jesus.

>Think about the person you know the best. How did you get to know them so well?

>Please read Matthew 9:14-15. Who does Jesus refer to Himself as in this passage?

>Please read Revelation 19:6-9. Who are believers in Christ referred to as in this passage?

>When believers finally get to be with Christ, what is the name of the celebration (v. 9)?

This is one time that I am so thankful I am a woman. All throughout the Bible God uses the image of marriage to represent His relationship to His people. All believers both men and women are called the bride of Christ. Men may have a harder time picturing themselves in this role, but as women, we easily embrace this concept. Those who have been a bride know what it is like to prepare for a wedding and the great anticipation that goes with it.

Have you ever wondered why we are called the bride of Christ and not the wife of Christ? What are characteristics of a bride?

The beginning of a relationship is new and exciting. It is all about getting to know the other person and discovering who they are. This is exactly what Jesus wants our relationship with Him to be like. He has left us His love letter and wants us to read it to get to know Him. The following verses describe God's love for you. Please read each verse, and write down the description of love that goes with each verse.

Isaiah 54:10, Psalm 63:3, Psalm 85:10-12, Romans 5:5, Ephesians 2:4-5 and 3:17-19.

Spend some time responding to God's love letter to you. Write Him words of love in return.

As a relationship progresses, routines set in and excitement diminishes. If I went on the same date with my husband every week, we would quickly get bored. Most of us do this same thing with God, and we expect to sense His presence and be wowed by Him. If you want to learn and see something new, you will have to do something new.

God's Word is the main tool we have for getting to know Him. It is probably a good idea to get to know your groom before the wedding. I want to give you a couple of ideas that could change the routine of your study time with Him. These are only my suggestions; you are free to think of other ideas. Try reading the Bible in a different translation than you are used to. Simply hearing new words can add new meaning. Try reading from a daily Bible that divides the Bible into readings for a whole year that include passages from the Old Testament, New Testament, Psalms, and Proverbs for each day. This is a great way to see how the whole Bible points to Jesus. Do your study time in a different location. Try studying outside, in the laundry room, or in a dry bathtub! It is okay if there are some distractions. Those distractions may lead you to new prayers. Instead of reading it yourself, try listening to the Word being read aloud. There are great products available that include sound effects and drama. Instead of reading a book of the Bible, try doing a word study. Look up all the verses on love, light, Heaven, or whatever subject interests you. God's Word is alive. Get excited again. Your groom is waiting!

What new approach are you going to try? Commit to doing something new this week.

Day 4
Our Father Which Art in Heaven

Well, the fact that you came back for today's lesson means I haven't totally scared you away. Changing up our routines is scary. Remember, our God is a God of new things so this will only help your relationship grow.

When I realized that God was telling me to take a break from dating relationships so I could focus on getting to know Him, I was fearful of being lonely. My need to be known was no different from anyone else's. I wanted someone with whom I could discuss my day and share my feelings. If I was going to head down this new path with Jesus, He would need to be the one I could share with. I had no idea where to start. One day on the way home from work, I turned off the radio and just started talking to Jesus as if I had just been picked up for a date. It was certainly awkward telling Jesus the events of my day since I was well aware He already knew. Did I mention I was talking to Him out loud? The popularity of hands-free devices saved me from the humiliation of other drivers thinking I had completely lost it. If I wanted this relationship to be authentic I needed it to feel real.

Thankfully dating relationships do not stay in the awkward stage. There is a natural progression of comfort and trust as you get to know someone. Each new situation teaches you something new about the other person. The more I had these "dates" with Jesus, the more I opened up. I learned to talk to Him as a friend and share my thoughts, emotions, and the very depth of my soul. And ladies this was not a one-sided conversation. By spending time in His Word and in prayer, I came to recognize His voice. Often when I am praying and sharing a concern with Jesus, a verse from the Bible will pop into my head. I will write it down and when I get home look up the passage. It always speaks to the exact need I have. I am not that smart. I know this is Jesus giving me the answer I need. Other times a song will come on the radio that just speaks to my heart. I receive this as a gift of love. God has also used other believers to confirm His plans to me. There have been times when I wasn't sure I knew what to do, and I would get a call out of the blue from someone that confirms what I was hearing from God. God is not silent, but it will take a personal relationship with Him so you can recognize His voice.

There are several examples of prayer in the Bible. Not only did Jesus model what prayer looks like to His disciples, but He directly shared with them a way they should pray. Please read Matthew 6:5-13.

What were some problems Jesus had with the Pharisees way of praying?

How did Jesus want His disciples to pray differently? What elements did Jesus want to be included in their prayers?

Many of you are so familiar with this prayer you didn't need to read the verses. Since Jesus gave this prayer as an example of how one should pray, many have interpreted that Jesus wanted us to say those exact words and never depart from them. Prayer is part of our personal relationship with Christ. Jesus had a problem with the Pharisees making a spectacle of prayer. Their point was to be seen by others rather than to share their heart with God. Jesus emphasized the importance of prayer as being personal. In this same passage, Jesus warned against meaningless repetition. Repetition can be a beautiful thing if the heart is still engaged in the prayer. The problem is when the heart and mind are not engaged with the words being said. Jesus said to pray "like this" in "this way" to show His disciples that there are some important elements to include in our prayers.

I want you to look closely at verses 9 through 13. Jesus starts the prayer by speaking to God in a personal way by calling Him "Father." Only those who have a relationship with God can call Him Father. Verse 9 is also filled with worship and reverence to who God is. In verse 10 Jesus acknowledges that God will keep His promises and yields all things to the will of God. Verse 11 asks God to provide for our daily needs and acknowledges our dependence on God. Verse 12 includes the importance of asking for forgiveness and repenting of our sins, while at the same time acknowledging that we have already forgiven others. The prayer ends with acknowledging our spiritual weakness and need for God to strengthen and protect us. Jesus was telling His disciples that all of these elements are important in prayer. A youth pastor once taught me a helpful acronym to remember these components of prayer. The acronym is PRAY. P stands for praise. R stands for repent. A stands for ask. Y stands for yield. This is not the same order of Jesus' prayer, but it includes all of the elements. It is easy to come to God in prayer when we have a need, but God wants it to be about our relationship. This example of prayer can help us have a more balanced approach to our prayers.

Another element of prayer that is seen in the Scripture is the many forms prayer can take. Please read the verses below and list all the diverse ways people prayed.

   1 Samuel 1:9-17, 1 Kings 8:54, Matthew 26:36-39, Luke 18:11, and John 17:1.

I hope you can see that prayer can be out loud or it can be silent. You can pray standing, on your knees, or on your face. Let the Holy Spirit lead you rather than a routine or custom. I have a few suggestions on new things to try during your prayer time. Try praying in a new posture. Try praying out loud with your eyes open. Go for a walk, and pray for all the people in every house you pass. You may not know the people, and this is a great opportunity to let the Holy Spirit guide your prayers. Go on a walk throughout your house, and pray in every room you come to. These are great things to do on your own or with your family. You can do these same things within your church building. I guarantee you will feel awkward trying something new. All first dates are awkward. The blessings come when the awkwardness turns into relationship.

What new approach are you going to try? Commit to doing something new this week.

Day 5
A Little More Undignified

When I was in college, I went on my first short-term mission trip. I spent three weeks in Costa Rica. I had been part of a church for four years by then, but I had never seen worship in another country. I was amazed at how differently worship and church routines could look outside of the norms I was used to. For starters, they began church in the morning, went home for a couple hours, and then came back in the evening. Often we would still be at church well past midnight. I attended two churches while I was there. One was a single cement room. The other was just a tin roof held up by wooden poles in the middle of a banana plantation. Along with the structure differences, their style of singing was also different. My home church sang praise songs so I was used to a little repetition, but nothing like what I would experience there. They would sing the same four simple lines over and over again. During my first week there, I was so annoyed by this. Couldn't they add a few more verses? I longed to worship the way I was used to. During one worship session, God opened my eyes to something I was missing. They were all singing in Spanish so I didn't pick up on this initially. Those leading worship would continue singing the same four verses, but everyone else in the congregation started singing their own words. They may have used some of the same words as the song, but the song just provided the melody for them to sing their own personal prayers to the Lord. I was overwhelmed by how beautiful it was to hear that many people singing their own special words to Jesus. Not only were their words unique but so were their actions. Some would stand, while others knelt. Some were dancing and clapping, while others sat praying. No one seemed to care what the others were doing. I have never seen such freedom in worship. When I returned home, I longed for the worship in Costa Rica.

King David certainly made great mistakes in his life, but He loved God with all his heart, and he knew what it meant to worship. David had a longing to bring the Ark of the Covenant back to Jerusalem. Unfortunately in his passion, he did not pay attention to the proper transportation of the ark written in the Law. When his first attempt failed, he did not give up but instead consulted God's Word and attempted it a second time.

> Please read 2 Samuel 6 and 1 Chronicles 15. Describe all the ways David worshiped God in these passages.

> What was David's response to Michal's disdain of his behavior (2 Samuel 6:21-22)?

In our worship to God, we are going to have to choose between the approval of other people or the approval of God. We cannot have both. David's worship to God included singing, playing instruments, dancing, offering sacrifices, and obeying God's law. His behavior may not have been thought appropriate for a king, but it was an appropriate response to his King. It is no wonder so many psalms of praise were written by this man.

When we think of worship, often what comes to mind first is singing. This is certainly one form of worship, but it is not the summation. Worship is giving praise and glory to God. It is acknowledging God above all else. It is giving God the credit. In our desire to know God more personally, we have to start taking things more personally. God has showered us with blessings all around. Our job is to notice them. One way I do this is by paying more attention to my five senses. What things around me do I see that I can praise God for? I love color. I call my house the "Skittle House" because each room is a different flavor. God could have made the world in black and white, but instead, He blessed us with color. Every time I see a particularly beautiful shade, whether in a sunset or in His Creation, I am reminded to praise Him. What about our sense of taste? Again God could have made food just for nutritional value and no flavor. Thank Him when you taste something wonderful. Apply this thought to your sense of smell, hearing, and touch. Just because things can be explained by science doesn't make them any less of a miracle. A rainbow may be water fragments reflecting sunlight, but God still created the formula. These are His personal gifts to all of us. How many gifts has He given us that we have failed to give Him the credit for?

Take a minute to notice your 5 senses. What can you praise God for right now?

Another way we can worship God is by acknowledging who He is. One activity I like to do with my kids is called ABC prayer. We take turns naming a characteristic of God that goes with each letter of the alphabet. For example, one person will start by saying, "A, our God is awesome." The next person will say, "B, my God is beautiful." We are always coming up with new attributes and characteristics. You can use this same practice as you read through your Bible. Start reading a passage until you come to a characteristic or attribute that starts with the letter A and then keep reading until you come to one for B.

Worship should be personal and fresh in the same way our study of Scripture and prayers should also be. Try worshiping with a different age group and a different style than you are used to. Find a church in your city that is from a different country. Call ahead and see if you can join them for a service. Your pastor may even have some relationships with some other churches and could recommend one. What would your worship look like if you were just a little more undignified? I'm not talking about being inappropriate or disrespectful. What would freedom look like in your worship?

What new approach are you going to try? Commit to doing something new this week.

Ladies I hope you have discovered some new ways to make your relationship with Jesus alive and new. He knows you completely and is delighted when you strive to know Him in return. He is not hidden, and your searching will reveal a much bigger God than you ever knew existed. Though I have forgotten much of the Spanish I once knew, I want to leave you today with the words of the song I will never forget. "Llename, llename Señor. Dame más, más de Tu amor. Yo tengo sed sólo de Ti. Llename Señor." Fill me, fill me Lord. Give me more, more of your love. I thirst for You alone. Fill me Lord.

Week 9
Fragile Jars of Clay

Day 1
Resurrection Power

  Day 2
  Removing the Mask

    Day 3
    Lean on Me

      Day 4
      Salt and Light

        Day 5
        Leaving a Legacy

If you were to look in my cupboards, you might think I didn't have much skill as a potter. I tend to keep all of the pieces that chip and crack since I can't give them away as gifts or sell them. Almost every kiln load has a least one piece that doesn't survive the heat. Working with such a fragile material can be frustrating, but the pieces that do survive are very durable and will last a very long time. We are also very fragile in nature. We can try to hide our weakness, but that doesn't make us any stronger. Our strength comes from who we rely on, not what we are. When we rely on the strength of Christ, we preserve truth and leave a legacy that generations can follow.

Session 9: Viewer Guide
Fragile Jars of Clay

Easily Broken

There are just as many verses in the Bible that show the making and shaping of pottery as there are of the fragile nature of pottery.

1. Our _____ are _____ to God (Isaiah 30:12-14, Jeremiah 25:34).

2. God desires that His _____ would lead to _____ (Jeremiah 18:7-8).

Preserving Qualities of Clay

1. Clay jars _____ what is kept _____ (Jeremiah 32:6-15).

2. Clay jars preserve the _____ of God (Jeremiah 29:10).

Treasure in Jars of Clay

1. We have a _____ to _____ (2 Timothy 1:14).

2. Our treasure is the _____ of Jesus Christ (2 Corinthians 4:5-12, 16-18).

3. Our _____ shows that the _____ is from God (vs. 7-9).

4. Outwardly we are _____ _____, yet inwardly we are being _____ (vs. 10-12, 16-18).

5. We can _____ in our weakness because God's _____ is made perfect (2 Corinthians 12:7-10).

Using our Weakness

1. With_____ ___ _____ the Israelites would _____ the battle (Judges 7:9-22).

Video discussion questions
1. Is it possible for you to see God's loving action in the destruction He pours out on His people? If you are able to see His love, what helps you to view it in this manner? If you are unable to see His love, what is holding you back?
2. God gave Jeremiah and the Israelites hope that their time in captivity would be limited, and they would return to their land. Has God ever sent you encouragement before a hard season? How did the encouragement impact you?
3. What are some ways we preserve our entrusted treasure, the knowledge of Jesus Christ?
4. Think of a time God used your weakness to show off His power. Please share it with the group.
5. Having weaknesses are not enjoyable. Our tendencies are to hide our weaknesses rather than show them off. How can we be vulnerable with our weaknesses so Christ's power may be known?
6. What is your favorite story in the Bible of God using weakness?

Videos are available for viewing at www.jennykaluza.com/the-potter-and-the-clay-videos.

Day 1
Resurrection Power

Though I tend to be a mushy romantic at heart, I love stories involving superheroes. I love the hidden powers they possess. I love listening to people discuss what super power they would like to have. There is something about being invincible that gives the viewer comfort. They may seem weak on the outside, but inside you know they have the strength to defeat the bad guy. The other element of the story that keeps the viewers hooked is that although they have a hidden strength, there is also a vulnerability to that strength. Superman's weakness is kryptonite, Spider-Man's is venom, and Iron Man has a weak heart. All superheroes have a weakness. Without their weakness, the story would be over in a matter of minutes. It is the vulnerability in the midst of great strength that draws us in.

All Christians have a superpower. Please read Ephesians 1:15-23.

> What is Paul's prayer for the believers (v. 16-17)?

> Why would a personal knowledge of God be important for understanding our spiritual blessings?

> What things did Paul want his readers to know (v. 18-19)?

> What acts were attributed to this power (v. 19-23)?

Now I know this was a letter Paul wrote to the people living in Ephesus, but I have to imagine if he was telling his listeners this message face to face, there would be a definite increase in volume behind these words. This is a message that needs to be shouted! There are so many things that we miss if we only have an intellectual knowledge of the Word. It is only through a personal relationship with Christ that one can experience the fullness of His blessings. Paul wanted us to know that anyone who has placed their faith in Jesus has the Holy Spirit within them. The power that is within a believer is the power of God. The power of God was powerful enough to raise Jesus from the dead, exalt Him above all authority, and appoint Jesus to be head of the church. Resurrection power is within believers in Christ! That does not mean the same power that was used to accomplish those mighty acts with Christ will do the same for us. We are not promised dominion and power. However, Paul is making the point that God's power is the same, it is just applied differently. Our hope, which is our salvation, is already secured because of the power of God. We have already won! Along with this hope, we have also been blessed with every spiritual blessing (Ephesians 1:3). We have been given so much more than we realize, and only by knowing God better and having the eyes of our heart enlightened can we truly appreciate the power we have been given. Paul was praying for this very thing for believers. I think it is appropriate to assume we should be praying that for ourselves as well. Pray to Jesus that you would know Him better, that the eyes of your heart would be enlightened. Please read Philippians 3:4-14.

Why did Paul start this passage by listing all his accomplishments?

What kinds of accomplishments do people boast in today? Before believing in Christ, what did you take confidence in?

Why is it necessary to lose the things of the flesh in order to gain the things of Christ?

What things did Paul want to know (v.10)?

What is our prize and how do we obtain it?

If anyone had reason to boast in their accomplishments, it was Paul. Before placing his faith in Christ, he did boast in all of his fleshly accomplishments. He would have been the envy of all his peers. We cannot rely on our own power and the power of God at the same time. Paul was aware that the power of God far exceeded any abilities he had on his own, and he chose to lose his fleshy dependence in exchange for the righteousness of God. Compared to what he gained, what he lost was only garbage. In comparison to knowing Christ, everything else has no value. Paul wanted to know the power of the resurrection that had raised Christ from the dead and that would one day raise all Christians as well. That knowledge comes from being conformed in Christ's image, dying to sins since Christ died for sins. Paul admitted that he was not made perfect yet, but he was striving toward that goal. He would receive his prize when at last Christ's resurrection power was realized in the resurrection of the saints.

Superheroes captivate our imagination because we long for something greater than ourselves and our own limited abilities. No matter what our outward boasting may look like, deep down we know how frail we are. The most incredible power available is realized in the hearts of every believer in Christ. That power is available to us when we rely on the ultimate Superhero, Jesus.

Right about now I think a theme song should start playing. Oh wait, He already has one. "To Him who sits on the throne and to the Lamb be praise and honor and glory and power, for ever and ever!" (Revelation 5:13)

Day 2
Removing the Mask

The terms teacher's pet, goody-goody, goody-two-shoes, and holier-than-thou are all used as derogatory terms for someone who has the air of being better than others. Many Christians have been called these names in their attempt to live a holy life. Certainly, we are called to be set apart from this world, but we are also supposed to draw people closer to Christ. How can we both live for Christ and create curiosity among the unsaved?

Having a reliance on our own abilities and strengths or relying on God's abilities and strength will not look a whole lot different to those around us without the ability to be vulnerable. Being vulnerable to others goes against every self-preservation bone in our body. When we are vulnerable, others can hurt us. If I was to ask you, "How are you doing today?" the most popular answer would be "fine." Christians are meant to have the joy of the Lord but always having a smiling face actually hinders our message. The joy of the Lord does not mean perpetual happiness. If we always appear to be invincible, how would anyone know that our strength is from Christ? We have to expose our weaknesses and needs in order to enlighten others to our source of strength.

Now there are still those who hate Jesus, and no amount of vulnerability will change that. That is part of the risk. We may expose our weaknesses to people who are unwilling to be changed. Our motivation to be vulnerable has to be to glorify God because that is the only thing we are guaranteed. Please read Luke 7:36-50.

> How was the woman who came to Jesus described? Why do you think people made this distinction?

> List all the actions of this woman. How do they compare with the Pharisee's?

> How do her actions reveal her vulnerability?

> Was this woman's sin greater than the other guests'? Did she have a greater need for forgiveness? Why was her behavior different from everyone else's?

I love the courage this woman displayed in her vulnerability. She did not have to come before Jesus in such a public place, but she was so overwhelmed with gratitude that she could not stay hidden. Her sins were laid bare for all to judge, but her forgiveness would also be for all to see. She came before Jesus in complete submission and humility, and He esteemed her for her actions. God is not ranking our sin based on severity. Her need for forgiveness was no different than anyone else's in that room. The difference was she realized the depth of her depravity and understood from what she had been saved.

One of the greatest blessings I received from working at a Christian homeless shelter was getting to witness firsthand the joy that comes when someone realizes they have been forgiven much. I heard about the women's painful pasts and sinful choices, and then I witnessed the change that comes from belief in Jesus. Because they had been surrounded by their sin, the realization of their forgiveness and freedom was easily evident. I have never seen such joyful worship as I did with those women. Their joy was contagious. It gave me an awareness of the forgiveness God had given me and a new appreciation for the price Jesus paid for me.

How can you gain a greater awareness of your sin and therefore a greater appreciation for your forgiveness?

How does having an accurate understanding of your sin create vulnerability with others and show off the strength of Christ?

If we hide our shortcomings, we mislead others into thinking we are incredibly put together on our own. Exposing our weakness goes against all human nature, but it's not our nature we want to reveal. By exposing our weakness, Christ's nature is revealed. We show others that even though life is hard and we fail, God's grace is sufficient, and He strengthens our otherwise weak nature.

Another part of being vulnerable is a willingness to submit to the authority placed in your life. Even Jesus chose to be vulnerable because He was submitting to God's plan. Please read Matthew 26:50-54.

Why did Jesus submit to God the Father rather than using the power at His disposal?

Even Jesus, who had every resource at His disposal chose to submit to the plan of God. What some would mock and claim as weakness on Christ's part, was the most powerful act in history. We allow others to see that power when we are honest about life. What do you struggle with? What areas of your life are still not all neat and put together? What causes you pain? What is your hope in the midst of pain? By learning to be real with others, we show others that our God is real.

So let's give this vulnerability thing a try. How are you doing today?

Day 3
Lean on Me

I am a planner, and I like to be prepared. I buy things on sale, and I stock up. I don't think I am unique in this. In fact, I think it is the American way. We plan for the future, and we know what our five-year plan is. Watch a television program for any length of time and you are bound to see a cereal stock-up sale or ads for retirement. We don't like surprises, and we desire stability. Being responsible is an admirable quality, but self-reliance easily sneaks up around the corner. Sometimes the only way we can learn God-dependence is to have all of our resources removed.

Please read Exodus 16. How much manna were the people to gather?

What was God's purpose is providing the manna (v. 4)? Also read Deuteronomy 8:3.

What was the result of their gathering (v.17-18)?

How is our tendency to stock up similar to the lack of faith of the Israelites?

Have you ever had a season in your life when you had to learn to rely on God's provisions? What did you learn?

What are some ways we can learn to be reliant on God without having all of our resources removed?

Please read Matthew 6:11. What kind of bread are we to ask for? Why?

I don't know about you, but I tend to like the yearly bread rather than the daily bread. As much as I would like to think I would have been obedient in my faith, I think I might have tried to hold on to my manna just one more day. Rather than rejoicing in the blessings of the Lord, I would have been left with the maggots. Isn't it just like us to want to maintain some illusion of control? Really that is all that it is, only an illusion. All it takes is one unexpected event, and all the best laid plans are ruined. Worrying takes away our ability to see the blessing.

God already knows we are frail and weak. He is just waiting for us to come to that conclusion as well. God longs to provide for us and be acknowledged as the one meeting our needs. What it really comes down to is do we believe God cares for us? In Matthew 6:26-30 Jesus pointed out the birds in the air and the lilies of the field to show that if God can care for the simple creatures of His creation, surely He cares much more for His children. God's mercies are new every morning! If we are only feasting on the yearly bread, we miss seeing the daily mercies.

One benefit of our weak nature is it teaches us a reliance on God. Another benefit is we learn the blessings of teamwork. Please read Exodus 17:8-13.

> Do you think God could have made Moses supernaturally strong that day instead of needing the help of Aaron and Hur? What were the added benefits of Moses' weakness?

> Please read Luke 10:1-11. Why do you think Jesus had the disciples pack so little for their journey? How were the people hosting the disciples also a part of their ministry?

The reality is if we could do it all on our own, we probably would. Needing the help of others makes us feel dependent and not capable. When we were remodeling our home, we tried to do everything on our own. It took multiple years and I'm sure much of our health. Looking back I'm not sure why we didn't reach out for help sooner, but it just didn't occur to us. We didn't want to be a burden to others. When some men in our church discovered that my husband was doing all this work by himself, they banded together for a work party. They helped install insulation, rip up flooring, and hammer boards together for a deck. They did more work together in a couple weekends than we could have done in a couple months. The other benefit was they formed relationships. These projects bonded them together and gave them all a feeling of accomplishment. When at last our house was finished, they all took pride in the finished result knowing they had a hand in it.

We were created for relationship with God and each other. Our weakness helps us to reach out to others and enjoy the blessing of fellowship. There is no shame in having needs. We were created that way. Jesus didn't send the disciples out with stomachs that would never get hungry. While they were ministering to others, the church was ministering to them. This is what true fellowship is all about.

> What is an area of your life that could use some teamwork? How could you reach out to others and share your need?

> What is a need of someone else's that you could help meet?

Week 9: Fragile Jars of Clay

Day 4
Salt and Light

Recently I went to my doctor, and he put me on a very restrictive diet to see if it would lead to improved health. One of the guidelines he gave me was to remove everything from my kitchen cupboards and pantry that had extremely long expiration dates. All of those items were sure to contain many preservatives and not something that would be beneficial for me. Preservatives may not be a great thing in our food, but they are excellent when paired with God's Word. Please read Matthew 5:13-16.

We have already discovered that clay pots were used to preserve treasures in Biblical times. That was not the only preserving agent of the day. Today we are going to study our call to be both salt and light in the world. We will look at both of these subjects separately. We will start by learning about salt.

> What do you use salt for in your house? What other uses are you aware of?

> According to Matthew 5:13 when is salt no longer useful?

> Please look back at Matthew 5:1. Who was Jesus teaching?

We are going to look at a couple other verses in the Bible that refer to salt.

> Please list every attribute of the salt you find in Leviticus 2:13, 2 Kings 2:19-22, and Job 6:6.

Hopefully, some of the qualities of salt you came up with are that it is used to preserve food, increase flavor, and purify. Salt was a well-known and used substance. It was used to add flavor just as we use it today, but it was also used to keep meat from decaying. God commanded the Israelites to put salt on their grain offerings as a sign of His everlasting covenant. Salt was thought to withstand fire, and it represented an eternal or lasting promise. Normally salt is thought to make water taste bad, but when Elisha added salt to the spring, the water was purified.

> Why would the qualities of salt be important qualities to see in Christians?

Two things occur when you add salt to food. One, it makes you thirsty. Two, it creates more flavor. Christians are to have qualities that draw the attention of the world around them and create a longing for what they have. The world should want to know why we are different. Salt also preserves, and Christians are to preserve God's truths and purify the world with their message of hope. Salt is meant to keep its flavor. Christians are meant to stay true to their purpose.

Being salt is one characteristic Christians are to have; the other is light. Throughout the Bible, light often represents God, while darkness represents evil. Please read John 8:12.

> What does Jesus call Himself, and what is the result if we follow Him?

> If we have the light of life, what should we do with it according to Matthew 5:14-16?

> What purposes do lights serve in your everyday life?

My family loves to go camping in the summer. We can spend hours sitting by the campfire at night playing games and telling stories. On more than one occasion I have got caught up in conversation only to realize my flashlight was still in my tent. Living in a city, it is hard to remember how dark night can get without all the city lights. A twenty foot walk to a tent suddenly turns into an obstacle course, and the tree roots are guaranteed the win. When at last the flashlight is turned on, the entire path is illuminated. We don't realize what a blessing light is until we are left in darkness. Once you have the light, it would be completely absurd to keep it hidden.

Jesus was making this point when He told His disciples that their light needed to be for all to see. The very nature of light is to shine. It radiates and gives direction. It points toward the proper path. Our light helps others see and praise God. When you have a light, you don't keep it a secret. God's message shouldn't be a secret either. Please read 2 Corinthians 4:6-7.

> What is the light contained in?

The Light is our treasure and that treasure is in jars of clay. Don't you just love how God's Word brings it all together! God's glory is placed in us and is meant to be in contrast to our weak bodies so that the source of the power cannot be hidden. We were meant to shine!

> Do you tend to hide your light? How could you reveal it more?

Day 5
Leaving a Legacy

My grandma, whom we call Bopie, was a force of change for my family. The generations that came before her were filled with all forms of abuse. In an effort to survive and make changes for herself, she left home at the age of 13. It was during World War II so she was able to find a job even though she was so young. She continued to support herself through her high school years and was able to graduate. She went on to get married and raise three children in a loving home even though she did not have an example to follow. Her skills were limited, and she made mistakes, but she did the best she could and prepared the next generation better than most would think possible. Her three children were equipped with more love and skill than the generation before them. Therefore, even more blessings were passed on to my generation. Though my grandma was certainly not perfect, she made a purposeful effort to stop the generational sin that had been passed down to her. Because of her actions, I was left with a legacy of blessings that I intend to pass on to my children.

What members of your family were elements of positive change?

Even though humans may be fragile in nature, we can be elements of great change. That change can have a positive or negative effect for generations to come. God desires that we would leave a legacy that will impact future generations and preserve the works of faith that have come before us. Much of Israel's history was to be passed down so that the future generation would know what marvelous things God had done for His people. Their celebrations were to be a time to remember and teach the next generation. Please read the following passages, and write down which events were to be told to the next generation and why.

Exodus 12:24-28 _____

Exodus 16:32 _____

Exodus 31:13 _____

Leviticus 23:39-43 _____

Joshua 4:1-7 _____

The intent of the traditions was to remember what God had done in the past and give confidence and faith in the future. If God had acted so mightily before, surely He could do it again. It was a time set aside to remember. Unfortunately, things that are often repeated lose their meaning and can become just a physical, going through the motions routine. If our heart is not engaged with the tradition, it becomes meaningless.

Do you have any traditions that help to renew your faith in God? What are some things you could do to preserve your journey with God so other generations could be blessed?

The Bible makes it very clear that the actions and choices we make affect not only ourselves but future generations to come. Please read Exodus 20:5-6.

What result did hating God or loving God have on future generations?

The concept of being cursed or blessed based on what the generations did before you can seem confusing and unfair. The good news is our choices can affect change. The history of Israel's kings is a perfect example of this. Under each section of Scripture, record what the king did right or wrong and the results of those actions.

1 Kings 3:2-3 _____ = 1 Kings 11:31-33 _____

1 Kings 14:21-24 _____ = 1 Kings 15:1-5 _____

2 Kings 15:32-35 _____ = 2 Kings 16:1-4 _____

In what ways do these kings represent God's judgment on sin and His blessings on righteousness handed down to the next generation?

Because of God's love for David and David's faithfulness to God, the nation of Judah would not be destroyed even though generations of kings would do evil. All of the verses we read today spoke of worshiping in the high places. The high places were places of worship dedicated to foreign gods. When Israel conquered the surrounding lands of their enemies, they were to destroy the high places. Rather than destroying them, we read of king after king failing to destroy the high places. Even though the kings themselves may have been righteous and followed after God, they left a place of temptation for future generations. I had to skip several generations based on time, but there is a long line on kings recorded in the books of 1 and 2 Kings that failed to remove the high places. Then, as we saw was the case with King Ahaz, the area of sin that his father failed to remove became the area of sin for him.

The most important legacy we can leave for future generations is our obedience and love for God. By putting an end to the sinful past that came before us and setting an example of righteousness, we leave a legacy of blessing for future generations. Each person is still responsible for their own actions, but we can blaze a trail that will help others make wise choices. Removing the areas of sin from our lives also removes the traps of sin for generations to come.

What do you want your legacy to be? What steps are you taking to ensure that future?

Week 10
Refiner's Fire

Day 1
Lion and the Lamb

    Day 2
I Am

        Day 3
Refined by Fire

            Day 4
Sacrifice of Praise

                Day 5
There Will Come a Day

Ladies I am honored that you would journey with me this long and make it to the final week of our study. I sit in awe over the places God has taken me and the lessons I have learned. The more I learn about Him, the more I am in wonder over His desire to use a common vessel such as myself. This study would not be complete without looking at the firing process the pieces go through in the kiln. This is what all the work and dedication is all about. Finally, we will have a finished, beautiful masterpiece! In order to make it to that final destination, the pieces have to be put in the fire. We also are refined by the fire. Only by knowing who God is and having a personal relationship with Him, will we trust Him enough to willingly go through the fire. God is glorified by our sacrifices and a glorious future awaits us. It will all be worth it! "Since ancient times no one has heard, no ear has perceived, no eye has seen any God besides you, who acts on behalf of those who wait for him" Isaiah 64:4.

Session 10: Viewer Guide
Refiner's Fire

The Masterpiece

1. You are Christ's _____ (Ephesians 2:10).

2. God's _____ _____ and _____ _____ are clearly seen in the creation of humankind (Romans 1:20).

Being Refined

1. We are refined through _____ (Isaiah 48:10).

2. God desires a _____ people who are able to bring offerings of _____ (Malachi 3:1-4).

3. Going through trials removes _____ that would otherwise _____ us (Revelation 3:17-18, Psalm 66:8-12).

4. Out of the fire comes a proven _____ of faith that _____ Jesus Christ (1 Peter 1:6-9).

5. The reality of Jesus' appearing will fill us with _____ _____ (1 Peter 1:7-8).

Video discussion questions

1. A masterpiece is an artist's best work. How does it make you feel to know God calls you His masterpiece?
2. In what ways have you seen God's eternal power and divine nature revealed in His creation?
3. Why do you think God uses suffering as part of His refinement process? Can you see a difference in your life between the things you learned in comfort and the things you learned through suffering?
4. Some people are destroyed by suffering and others are refined. What do you think makes the difference in the outcome?
5. How do we know when God's refining process is finished?
6. Have you ever had moments of praising God in the pain? What allowed you to praise in that moment? What about after the pain? Were you able to look back and praise Him? What evidence allowed the change in response?
7. What have been the results of your refining moments? What beliefs were solidified for you?
8. Looking back over the last ten weeks, what lessons are you going to take with you from the clay?

Videos are available for viewing at www.jennykaluza.com/the-potter-and-the-clay-videos.

Day 1
The Lion and the Lamb

I will never forget the moment I told my mom I was going to marry Zach. As I mentioned before, we did not have a typical dating relationship. We knew before our first date that we would be married. God provided many miracles in both our lives to confirm this. I was nervous to tell my parents about my experiences with God because I knew it was not normal. Rather than doubting my experiences, my mom said, "You have always believed in a big God." I had to sit back and ponder that comment. She was right, I always had believed in a big God. I didn't see the point of believing in a small god. If God wasn't exactly who He said He was, what would be the point of following Him? If I could do everything myself, why would I need God? I expect God to do great things because He is great. If I catch myself putting limits on what God is capable of, I pray to God to expand my boundaries. I'm not asking for a larger piece of land, I am asking for a greater understanding of who He is.

We can know God's character and nature from what He reveals about Himself in the Bible. If we don't know who He is, it will be impossible to trust Him. The refining process can be painful and scary. In order to endure the process and remain faithful until Christ returns, we have to know our God. Please read Isaiah 31:4, Hosea 5:14, 11:9-10, and Revelation 5:5.

What attributes come to mind when you think about a lion?

What truths of God and His character are revealed in these verses?

Please read John 1:29-30, 1 Corinthians 5:7, Revelation 5:12, and Revelation 7:17. What attributes come to mind when you think about a lamb?

What truths of God and His character are revealed in these verses?

What would some problems be with a God who was all lion?

What would some problems be with a God who was all lamb?

Week 10: Refiner's Fire

Please read Revelation 6:16. What action is attributed to the Lamb in this verse?

I am so thankful that the Lamb of God can also roar. You would never expect that the Lamb would be capable of wrath. That's the problem with trying to fit God into a nice little box, He doesn't fit. Our goal is not to make Him conform to the image we are comfortable with but to know Him as He really is. It is easier to identify with the Lamb. A lamb is safe and gentle, and it draws you near. A lion is scary, unpredictable, and wild. There is also another side of a lion we may not be considering. In the verses that referred to God as a lion, He showed how He is protective, powerful, triumphant, unafraid, willing to do battle, and calls with an identifiable voice. Those are all characteristics I am thankful my God has. He is willing to fight for you! Our God is both the Lion and the Lamb. All of the attributes of God are necessary because He is all things. We cannot accept one without the other. Though we may not understand how all these things can coexist within our God, one thing we do know is our God is always good.

My favorite image of this comes from the book *The Lion, the Witch and the Wardrobe* by C.S. Lewis. "Is-is he a man?" asked Lucy. "Aslan a man!" said Mr. Beaver sternly. "Certainly not. I tell you he is the King of the wood and the son of the great Emperor-beyond-the-Sea. Don't you know who is the King of Beasts? Aslan is a lion-the Lion, the great Lion." "Ooh!" said Susan, "I'd thought he was a man. Is he quite safe? I shall feel rather nervous about meeting a lion." "That you will, dearie, and no mistake," said Mrs. Beaver; "if there's anyone who can appear before Aslan without their knees knocking, they're either braver than most or else just silly." "Then he isn't safe?" said Lucy. "Safe?" said Mr. Beaver; "don't you hear what Mrs. Beaver tells you? Who said anything about safe? 'Course he isn't safe. But he's good. He's the King, I tell you."[1]

In order to go through the fire and come out refined, you must believe God is good. Fire will either destroy you, or it will make you stronger. You will not stay the same. There is no way I can convince you of God's goodness. I could take you to all the verses in the Bible that say God is good, but until you believe it for yourself, it will make no difference. The way we know God is good is the same way we believe in others' goodness. We go by their behavior in the past and trust they will stay true to their character in the future. The difference with God is that not only do we have our own personal experience with God to go by, but we also have the Bible as a reference to see how God kept His word with others. It will still come down to an issue of faith. Are you going to believe God and trust that He is good? One benefit of going through the fire is it clarifies our beliefs. All doubts are brought to the surface, and our faith will be revealed.

In what ways has God showed His goodness to you in the past? Do your experiences help you to trust Him in the future?

In the midst of going through the fire, what truths can you cling to so you are refined rather than damaged?

Day 2

I Am

Our son has struggled with his speech and works hard in therapy to try to learn things that come naturally to others. It wasn't until he turned three that he was finally able to say his name. In an effort to get him to practice saying everyone's name, we would play a game. I would point to someone in the car and say, "Who's this?" He would then happily respond by attempting to say the person's name. When I would point to him and say, "Who's this?" He would laugh and say, "Me." He never attempted to say his name but would always refer to himself as "Me." He would often say, "Me turn" and "Me do it." It was as if he was saying, "You know who I am, I'm just me."

I love hearing all the names of God compiled into one long list. So much of who God is and His nature is revealed in the names others have called Him or names He calls Himself. My favorite name of all is "I Am." I like to think of this name with the same meaning my son had when he called himself "Me." I like to think of the name "I Am" as the compilation of all the names of God. Please read Exodus 3:13-15.

> How does God further explain the name "I Am" in verse 15?

God wanted the Israelites to know that the God who had always been in existence was still their God. He let them know that the same God who had been a personal and covenant making God to Abraham, Isaac, and Jacob was also pursuing a relationship with them. All of this was summed up in the name that all generations would call Him, "I Am." This name shows that God is unchanging. His stability throughout the generations leads to an ability to trust Him and gives us a confidence that He can be known. Because He has worked for the good of His people, we know He is also working for our good. The journey, though painful, revealed God's purpose and care for His people.

This is not the only name of God that expresses His ever-present nature. Please read Revelation 1:7-8 and 22:12-13.

> Please list all the names for Jesus mentioned in these verses.

> What meaning is communicated by these names?

Alpha and Omega are the first and last letters of the Greek alphabet. The names "The Alpha and the Omega" and "The First and the Last" both represent the order of all things. The name "The Beginning and the End" represents an image of time. He is the God who is, and who was, and who is to come. Nothing is outside of His realm.

Week 10: Refiner's Fire

What name of God has special meaning to you? How did you come to know Him by that name?

Some names God gives Himself; other names of God come from people's interactions with Him. Please read Genesis 16:7-13.

What name did Hagar give the Lord? What experiences prompted this name?

Based on what you are going through right now, what name would you give God?

Often the names that mean the most to us are the names that are associated with a personal experience with God. Hagar learned that God is a personal God because He saw her misery, and He responded. God has the beautiful ability to meet us exactly where we are at. You can pretty well count that there is a name for God to go with the need He is meeting.

One of the names of God that is the most personal to me is the Potter. This name has personal meaning to me because of the character of God it represents. I feel like I get to know a new dimension of who He is each time I learn a new name. There is still one name that we are all yet to learn. Please read Revelation 19:11-13.

Why do you think one name of Jesus has remained hidden from us?

Oh, how I long to know that name! A name that no one has defiled or cursed. A name that only Jesus knows. Until we learn that precious name, we have a long list of names we can call Him.

Advocate, Almighty, Alpha & Omega, Anchor, Ancient of Days, Anointed One, Beloved, Bread of Life, Bridegroom, Carpenter, Chief Cornerstone, Christ, Comforter, Daystar, Deliverer, Emmanuel, Everlasting Father, First Born, God, Good Shepherd, Great High Priest, Head of the Church, Highest, Holy One, I Am, Image of God, Immanuel, Judge, King of the Jews, King of Kings, Lamb of God, Light of the World, Living Water, Lord God Almighty, Lord of Lords, Mediator, Man of Sorrows, Master, Messiah, Only Begotten, Physician, Prince of Peace, Prophet, Rabbi, Redeemer, Rock, Root of Jesse, Ruler of the Earth, Savior, Shepherd, Son of God, Suffering Servant, Teacher, The Amen, The Faithful & True Witness, The Author and Finisher of our Faith, The Bright Morning Star, The Chief Apostle, The Lamb Who Was Slain, The Lion of the Tribe of Judah, The Pioneer and Perfecter of our Faith, The Resurrection and the Life, The Root & Descendant of David, The Stone Whom the Builders Rejected, The Word, My Jesus!

Day 3
Refined by Fire

For the majority of us, our refining moments will be in a figurative fire rather than a literal one. But for three men, their refining moment was both figurative and literal. Because the nation of Judah had continued to ignore the warnings of God to repent and obey God's laws, God allowed the nation of Judah to be taken into captivity by the Babylonians. While in Babylon, some of the Jews were selected for the king's service. Three of those men were Shadrach, Meshach, and Abednego. Please read Daniel chapter 3.

What was the command given in verses 4-6?

Why is fear such a powerful motivator? Has fear ever motivated you to do something you normally wouldn't do?

I'm not sure if these three men were the only ones to disobey the orders of the king, but they are the only ones mentioned. We know by the positions listed of who was gathered for this ceremony that it would have been a very large crowd. I cannot imagine the pressure they faced to follow the crowd. There are all sorts of ways you could justify this behavior. You could tell yourself, "I'm just going to go through the motions, but in my heart I won't worship so I'll still be obeying God." You could tell yourself, "God wants me to obey the authorities placed over me. This king has been placed over me so I will honor my God by obeying this king." The point is there are many ways to justify our behavior so we can feel good about following the crowd.

How did Shadrach, Meshach, and Abednego respond to the king's command (v. 8-12)?

The king gives the men a second chance to obey him. How do they respond the second time (v. 16-18)?

How does their refusal the second time show even more resolve than the first?

The first time Shadrach, Meshach, and Abednego disobeyed the orders of the king it was in a large crowd, and their actions may have gone unnoticed. The second time, they stood before the king, and he gave them a direct order. I wish the thoughts of each man were recorded in these passages. I'm not sure how long this gold statue took to make. Was everyone talking about it before it went up? Did these three men already have a good idea that this was to be an idol made for worshipping? Had they already made a pact with each other that they would not worship it? Unfortunately, these are details we don't know in the story, but one thing we do know is these men had already resolved what was right and wrong before their faith was ever tested. We do not see them hesitating or wavering the moment the test was presented. They were not scrabbling to determine their beliefs in the moment of crisis. They knew God's laws and that superseded any king's law.

If we wait until the moment our fiery trial arrives to make up our mind how we will respond, we are not likely to be very successful. Our character has to be well established before our trials so the trials only serve to prove our character, not determine it.

> What are some ways can you establish your character before you are tested?

> Was Shadrach, Meshach, and Abednego's response to the king based on the belief that they would be delivered from the trial (V. 17-18)?

> What was the result of their disobedience to the king (V. 19-23)?

Putting your faith in God does not exempt you from suffering. These men were prepared for the consequences of their disobedience to the king. As they acknowledged, God is certainly capable of delivering us from all trials. However, we do not know what purposes God is working with each trial so it is impossible to know the outcome. Our obedience needs to be based on more than an escape from pain. God may deliver us from a trial, or He may ask us to go through it.

> What was Nebuchadnezzar's response to God saving Shadrach, Meshach, and Abednego and their obedience to God (V. 28-29)?

> What are some purposes God might have for you to go through a trial?

When others watch us being refined by our God, it should lead to an acknowledgment of the Most High God and give glory to Him alone. We do not know Nebuchadnezzar's heart at this moment, but we do know he had to acknowledge that there was no god like the Most High God! Suffering reveals our character like nothing else can. When gold comes out of a fire, no one can question the awesomeness of our God.

Day 4
Sacrifice of Praise

My favorite times of praising the Lord are when I am cooking. I love to turn the music up loud and just get lost in praise. I am already a messy cook so this just adds to the experience. These moments of praise are always associated with joy. I am singing because I am overflowing with love for Jesus. Although I know Jesus loves these moments in our relationship, they do not carry the same significance as the moments when I praise Him in pain. For some background information on today's lesson please read 1 Samuel 23:14-20.

What events are happening in the life of David? Where is he living?

Along with Saul, what other concerns did David have during this time (V. 19-20)?

According to The Bible Knowledge Commentary, David fled from Saul's house around the age of 20 and hid in the wilderness for approximately 10 years.[2] During this ten year time in the wilderness, Saul was constantly pursuing David and attempting to kill him. Saul knew that his dynasty was threatened by the existence of David. David was not free from harm until Saul was killed.

Ten years is a long time to hide and endure persecution. I'm sure there had to be moments when David did not think he would survive. David's time in the wilderness was not wasted time though. God was using this experience to shape David into the king he would one day be. Please read Psalm 54 which David wrote during this time in the wilderness.

By what means does David ask God to save him? What do the first two verses reveal about David's knowledge of God?

What is David's current situation at this time of prayer (V.3)?

Verses 4 and 5 contain a level of confidence in God's abilities. Why do you think David had confidence in a hopeless situation?

How did David characterize his praise in verse 6?

David called on the name of God to save him! He knew that who God is and what He has done are all represented in His name. Because of his relationship with God, he could already attest to God's power and ability to hear and act. David was praying in a time of urgent need. He was afraid for his life. David could pray boldly for help because he had a personal relationship with God. He put all his confidence in God's abilities because he knew that was the only thing sustaining him. Based on what David already knew about God, he chose to praise Him in the midst of his trial. His praise was based on who God was, not what was happening. He called his praise a freewill offering. Freewill offerings were part of the sacrificial system of the Israelites. They were offered voluntarily and were associated with rejoicing before the Lord. David praised God not because it was required, but because God was still the same God regardless of his circumstances and therefore worthy of praise. David did not know the outcome of his circumstance at his time of praise. David was confident of God's deliverance, but that was only based on God's past protection. He would still have to wait for his current deliverance.

Why would praising in a time of pain be of special significance?

Have you ever praised God during a time of pain? How did it differ from joyful praise?

Please read Hebrews 13:11-16. What things are considered sacrifices of praise (v. 15-16)?

Why are those things considered sacrifices?

The writer of Hebrews starts out by mentioning the sacrifices made on the Day of Atonement under the old sacrificial system. Jesus' suffering and death on the cross had taken the place of the old system, and it is now His life and death that make people holy. Animal sacrifices are no longer needed. Instead, sacrifices that are pleasing to God are the sacrifices of praise, of doing good, and sharing with others. These are the things that God desires.

These things are sacrifices because there is still a cost. The sacrifice of praise mentioned here is an acknowledgment of who God is and a thankful attitude regardless of circumstances. The sacrifice is that we have to put away our selfishness and personal desires in order to have a heart of praise. Doing good and sharing with others is a sacrifice. We may not feel like giving of ourselves to someone in need, but that is why it is a sacrifice. God is pleased when we do these things. Only when we have a history of walking with God can we praise Him in the pain. It is then that we can rely on who He is, not what is happening.

"You do not delight in sacrifice, or I would bring it; you do not take pleasure in burnt offerings. My sacrifice, O God, is a broken spirit; a broken and contrite heart you, God, will not despise" Psalm 51:16-17.

Day 5
There Will Come a Day

Ladies, I know the things we have studied during the last ten weeks are difficult topics. I did not write these words lightly. It is only because of the hope we have set before us that I ask you to endure. There will be a day in our future that will make all of these struggles nothing more than a distant memory, and our reward will at last be a reality. Until that day we need to strive toward the holiness Christ is creating in us. Please read 2 Peter 3:1-15.

What will the mockers say about Christ's second coming (v.3-4)? Have you already heard similar comments regarding your faith?

What are two reasons Christ's return may seem delayed to some (v. 8-9)?

How will the day of the Lord come?

How should we live until Christ returns (v. 11 and 14)? How might this way of living speed His return (v. 12)?

What are we looking forward to (v. 13)?

There will always be people who make fun of our beliefs and do not see that their behavior is leading to destruction. These are the same types of people who did not heed the warnings of the flood or the messages of the prophets. God is purposeful in everything He does. What some see as Him delaying, is all a part of His plan. He has a different concept of time than we do, and He is giving everyone a chance to hear and accept the gospel message. Make no mistake, when the time comes for His return, it will be swift and all will take notice. Our goal is to continue living holy and blameless lives until Christ returns, allowing Him to continue the good work started in us at the moment of our salvation. By living holy lives, praying, and witnessing to others we can help lead others to repentance. The more the gospel is spread, the faster Christ will return. We are not to look forward to the destruction of the Earth, but we know it must come. Our salvation is a certainty so we have no fear in the future, but we look forward to a new heaven and a new earth where righteousness will reign.

Three times in this passage Peter mentions our attitude toward these future events. He uses the original Greek word *prosdokao*. It means "to look for, wait for, and to expect."[3]

Look back at verses 11 through 14. In what ways do your actions show you are expecting Christ's promises to be fulfilled?

Please read Revelation 21:1-7. Why will there be no more pain (v. 4-5)?

Who will inherit this new place (v. 7)?

Continue by reading the rest of the chapter. What are you most looking forward to in Heaven?

How can these promises help you to endure the struggles of this life?

The former things, the things that now cause us so much pain and heartache, are not eternal things. There will be an end to all our suffering. We will get to experience a kind of intimacy with God like we have never known before. Our relationship, which is currently hindered by the presence of sin, will be made complete. Jesus will make all things new, and this new perfect place will be filled with peace. We will win! We will be victorious!

Whew! What a process we have been through! All the details of your life were purposefully planned before your creation. God has worked diligently to center you and to teach you to abide in Him. His Holy Spirit exposes your sin so it can be removed from your life. He is molding and shaping you into the image of Christ. He works with you to remove all of the burdens that are weighing you down, in order to create a vessel He can use for any good work. He never wastes a moment in your life. As His precious child, He has asked you to bring His love to others. He knows you so completely that you are engraved on to the palms of His hands, and He desires for you to know Him in return. He has made you fragile on purpose so that His strength could be shown through you. And at last, He has refined you. The refining process is difficult but something we all must go through. When you are refined, you are forever changed.

"Yet you, LORD, are our Father. We are the clay, you are the potter; we are all the work of your hand" Isaiah 64:8.

Endnotes

Week 1
1. "Hebrew Lexicon :: H6213 (KJV)." Blue Letter Bible. Sowing Circle. Web. 5 Sep, 2014.
2. "Hebrew Lexicon :: H1254 (KJV)." Blue Letter Bible. Sowing Circle. Web. 5 Sep, 2014.
3. "Hebrew Lexicon :: H3335 (KJV)." Blue Letter Bible. Sowing Circle. Web. 5 Sep, 2014.
4. "Hebrew Lexicon :: H1129 (KJV)." Blue Letter Bible. Sowing Circle. Web. 5 Sep, 2014.

Week 2
1. "Hebrew Lexicon :: H3201 (KJV)." Blue Letter Bible. Sowing Circle. Web. 5 Sep, 2014.
2. John F. Walvoord and Roy B. Zuck, *The Bible Knowledge Commentary: Old Testament* (Colorado Springs, CO: David C. Cook, 1983), 81.
3. Ibid., 81.
4. "Greek Lexicon :: G3306 (KJV)." Blue Letter Bible. Sowing Circle. Web. 5 Sep, 2014.

Week 3
1. "Greek Lexicon :: G2476 (KJV)." Blue Letter Bible. Sowing Circle. Web. 5 Sep, 2014.
2. William Fay and Ralph Hodge, *Share Jesus Without Fear* (Nashville, TN: LifeWay Press 1997).

Week 4
1. Vine, W. "Dictionaries :: Conformed, Conformable." Blue Letter Bible. Sowing Circle. 24 Jun, 1996. Web. 5 Sep, 2014.
2. Easton, Matthew. "Dictionaries :: Sovereignty." Blue Letter Bible. Sowing Circle. 24 Jun, 1996. Web. 5 Sep, 2014.
3. "Greek Lexicon :: G2233 (KJV)." Blue Letter Bible. Sowing Circle. Web. 5 Sep, 2014.
4. Viktor E. Frankl, *Man's Search for Meaning* (Beacon Press, 2006).

Week 5
1. John F. Walvoord and Roy B. Zuck, *The Bible Knowledge Commentary: New Testament* (Colorado Springs, CO: David C. Cook, 1983), 487.

Week 6
1. "Greek Lexicon :: G2288 (KJV)." Blue Letter Bible. Sowing Circle. Web. 5 Sep, 2014.

Week 7
1. Vine, W. "Dictionaries :: Merciful (Adjective, and Verb, to Be), Mercy (Noun, and Verb, to Have, Etc.)." Blue Letter Bible. Sowing Circle. 24 Jun, 1996. Web. 5 Sep, 2014.
2. "Greek Lexicon :: G25 (KJV)." Blue Letter Bible. Sowing Circle. Web. 5 Sep, 2014.

Week 8
1. "Hebrew Lexicon :: H3045 (KJV)." Blue Letter Bible. Sowing Circle. Web. 5 Sep, 2014.
2. John F. Walvoord and Roy B. Zuck, *The Bible Knowledge Commentary: New Testament* (Colorado Springs, CO: David C. Cook, 1983), 536.

Week 10
1. C. S. Lewis, *The Lion, the Witch, and the Wardrobe* (New York, N.Y. : Macmillan, 1950).
2. John F. Walvoord and Roy B. Zuck, *The Bible Knowledge Commentary: Old Testament* (Colorado Springs, CO: David C. Cook, 1983), 450.
3. "Greek Lexicon :: G4328 (KJV)." Blue Letter Bible. Sowing Circle. Web. 5 Sep, 2014.

Made in the USA
Middletown, DE
31 December 2018